THE *Lyric* LIBRARY

Broadway

Volume I

Complete Lyrics for 200 Songs
From 109 Musicals

HAL•LEONARD®

Other books in *The Lyric Library*:

Broadway Volume II

Christmas

Classic Rock

Contemporary Christian

Country

Early Rock 'n' Roll

Love Songs

Pop/Rock Ballads

ISBN 0-634-04479-6

Visit Hal Leonard Online at
www.halleonard.com

Preface

What would the history of popular song be without the Broadway musical? And what would the Broadway musical be without the master lyric writers who found the seemingly inevitable words that sit on the notes of timeless tunes? The list goes on and on of great stage lyricists who defined the sensibilites of their times: Irving Berlin, the team of Betty Comden and Adolph Green, Fred Ebb, Ira Gershwin, Oscar Hammerstein, Lorenz Hart, Jerry Herman, Alan Jay Lerner, Frank Loesser, Cole Porter, Tim Rice, Stephen Sondheim…

Lyrics in the British influenced operetta era on Broadway before the 1920s tended to be artificial, purplish and high-flown. In contrast, the lyrics of Lorenz Hart and Cole Porter, among others, took American vernacular speech and turned it into comfortable, casual verse. The best standards from musicals written between the two world wars remain fresh even today, not only due to unforgettable melodies, but also because the lyrics cleverly capture and condense everyday, on-the-street American language.

Most of the mature book musicals of the 1940s, 1950s and 1960s, by Rodgers & Hammerstein, Lerner & Loewe, Frank Loesser, Jerry Herman and other major figures, produced songs that were more specific to character and plot. That didn't prevent many of them from becoming hits: the sensibly earnest "I've Grown Accustomed to Her Face" from *My Fair Lady*, the glamorous yearnings of "Make Someone Happy" from *Do Re Mi*, the wistful nostalgia of "How Are Things in Glocca Morra" from *Finian's Rainbow*, and the manic hope of "Luck Be a Lady Tonight" from *Guys and Dolls*, among dozens of examples.

A modern, urban point of view emerged in Broadway lyrics of the 1960s and 1970s, especially from top talents such as Fred Ebb and Stephen Sondheim. A few years later, grand romanticism came to the stage in the mega-hits *The Phantom of the Opera* and *Les Misérables*, with sweeping lyrics in broad, expressive strokes.

New writers continue to find fresh turns of phrase to mirror contemporary thought as the musical moves ahead in a new century. And the success of professional revivals proves that a well-crafted, inspired and classic show has timeless appeal.

The houselights still dim all over the world every night as the first notes of a musical are heard, and the dawn of every new experience in the theatre has the promise of "Oh, What a Beautiful Mornin'."

Contents

Broadway
Volume I

Adelaide's Lament

By Frank Loesser

from *Guys and Dolls*

The av'rage unmarried female,
Basically insecure,
Due to some long frustration may react
With psychosomatic symptoms
Difficult to endure,
Affecting the upper respiratory tract.

In other words,
Just from waiting around
For that plain little band of gold,
A person can develop a cold.
You can spray her wherever you figure
The streptococci lurk,
You can give her a shot for whatever
    she's got,
But it just won't work.
If she's tired of getting the fish-eye
From the hotel clerk,
A person can develop a cold.

Spoken:
It says here,

Sung:
The female remaining single,
Just in the legal sense,
Shows a neurotic tendency. See note.
(Spoken) Note:
(Sung) Chronic, organic syndromes,
Toxic or hypertense,
Involving the eye, the ear, and the nose,
    and throat.

In other words,
Just from worrying whether the wedding is
    on or off,
A person can develop a cough.
You can feed her all day
With the Vitamin A and the Bromo Fizz,
But the medicine never gets anywhere near
Where the trouble is.
If she's getting a kind of a name for herself,
And the name ain't "his,"
A person can develop a cough.

And furthermore, just from stalling and
    stalling,
And stalling the wedding trip,
A person can develop La grippe.
When they get on the train for Niag'ra,
And she can hear church bells chime,
The compartment is air conditioned,
And the mood sublime.
Then they get off at Saratoga
For the fourteenth time,
A person can develop La grippe,
(Hm!) La grippe,
La post nasal drip,
With the wheezes and the sneezes
And a sinus that's really a pip!
From a lack of community property
And a feeling she's getting too old,
A person can develop a bad, bad cold.

All Alone

Words and Music by Irving Berlin

from *Music Box Revue of 1924*

Just like a melody that lingers on,
You seem to haunt me night and day.
I never realized till you had gone,
How much I cared about you.
I can't live without you.

All alone,
I'm so all alone.
There is no one else but you.
All alone
By the telephone
Waiting for a ring,
A ting-a-ling.
I'm all alone
Every evening
All alone.
Feeling blue,
Wondering where you are,
And how you are
And if you are
All alone too.

Adventure

Words by Betty Comden and Adolph Green
Music by Jule Styne

from *Do Re Mi*

Hubie:
You should have married Seymour Brilkin.
A better life you would be leading.
Respectable, secure,
So comf'table and sure,
A regular Missus counsellor at law.
You should have married Seymour Brilkin.
Down on his knees you heard him pleading.
He tore his hair and cried,
Yet you turned him aside.
Why didn't you listen to your maw?

Kay:
Ah yes, ah yes, I'd have two fur coats,
And a black beaded dress,
Two cars,
Two houses,
Two safe deposit boxes,
Two poodles,
And oodles of dripping silver foxes.

Hubie:
You should have married Seymour Brilkin,
Oh, what a lush life it would be.
You'd be living high.
Kay:
So kindly tell me why,
The wealthy Missus Brilkin is jealous of me.

'Cause I've got adventure, adventure,
With you ev'ry day is an adventure.
I wake with the dawn and before I can yawn,
There's a knock at the door.
Who knows what lies in store?
Are you under arrest?
Have we been dispossessed?
Will we find ourselves out on the street?

Yes, I've got adventure, adventure,
With you, let me say, it's an adventure.
So dear Missus Brilkin,
Go keep all your silken and satin and mink
    lingerie.
My life is a ball,
It's the "Perils of Pauline" with my name up
    on the marquee!
It's adventure for me!

Hubie:
You should have married Sheldon Miller,
And have the million things you're missing.
A dope, a brain of wood,
In plastics he made good,
So you could be Missus "Plastic Garment
    Bag."
You should have married Sheldon Miller.
The ground you walked on he was kissing.
But you told him, "Drop dead!"
And you took me, instead.
If you were his wife, your mom could brag.

Kay:
Ah so, ah so, I'd have full-time maids,
And an old French chateau,
Two yachts,
Two airplanes,
A home with two golf courses,
French labels,
And stables of fiery racing horses.

Hubie:
You should have married Sheldon Miller.
Oh, what a lush life it would be.
(Spoken) Built of solid gold,
Kay (Sung):
So why is it I'm told
The horsy Missus Miller is jealous of me?

'Cause I've got adventure, adventure,
With you, may I say, it's an adventure.
You've passed a bum check and the guy's on
    your neck,
So we dash out of town for a spree.
The place that we stay is in Far Rockaway,
With a heavenly view of the sea.
But the bill soon arrives, so we run for
    our lives,
Out the window, by dark, we continue
    our lark.
We drop to the streets on a ladder of sheets,
It's an unobserved drop, all except for
    one cop.

We flee, hand in hand, down the damp
    midnight sand,
By a great piece of luck, there's the back
    of a truck.
It bumps us to town,
I'm still in my nightgown.

Well, the weekend's been chic,
And it's tune in next week.
So dear Missus Miller,
Go keep your chinchilla,
'Cause even if Sheldon were free,
I'd give up each ruby and stick to my Hubie.
It's adventure,
Adventure, for me.

Ah well, Seymour Brilkin,
Ah well, Sheldon Miller,
Oh well, what's a girl gonna do?
Hubie Cram, I love you.

All at Once You Love Her

Lyrics by Oscar Hammerstein II
Music by Richard Rodgers

from *Pipe Dream*

You start to light
Her cigarette
And all at once
You love her.
You've scarcely talked,
You've scarcely met,
But all at once
You love her.

You like her eyes,
You tell her so.
She thinks you're wise
And clever.
You kiss goodnight
And then you know
You'll kiss goodnight
Forever!
You wonder where your heart can go
And all at once you know.

All I Ask of You

Music by Andrew Lloyd Webber
Lyrics by Charles Hart
Additional Lyrics by Richard Stilgoe

from *The Phantom of the Opera*

Raoul:
No more talk of darkness,
Forget these wide-eyed fears:
I'm here, nothing can harm you,
My words will warm and calm you.
Let me be your freedom;
Let daylight dry your tears:
I'm here, with you, beside you,
To guard you and to hide you.

Christine:
Say you love me every waking moment;
Turn my head with talk of summertime.
Say you need me with you now and always;
Promise me that all you say is true;
That's all I ask of you.

Raoul:
Let me be your shelter;
Let me be your light.
You're safe,
No one will find you;
Your fears are far behind you.

Christine:
All I want is freedom,
A world with no more night;
And you, always beside me,
To hold me and to hide me.

Raoul:
Then say you'll share with me one love, one
    lifetime;
Let me lead you from your solitude.
Say you need me with you,
Here beside you.
Anywhere you go, let me go too.
Christine, that's all I ask of you.

Christine:
Say you'll share with me one love, one life-
    time;
Say the word and I will follow you.

Together:
Share each day with me, each night, each
    morning.

Christine:
Say you love me!

Raoul:
You know I do.

Together:
Love me, that's all I ask of you.
Anywhere you go, let me go too.
Love me, that's all I ask of you.

Always True to You in My Fashion

Words and Music by Cole Porter

from *Kiss Me, Kate*

Oh, Bill,
Why can't you behave?
Oh, why can't you behave?
How in hell can you be jealous,
When you know, baby, I'm your slave?
I'm just mad for you,
And I'll always be,
But naturally,

If a custom tailored vet
Asks me out for something wet,
When the vet begins to pet,
I cry, "Hooray!"
But I'm always true to you, darlin',
  in my fashion,
Yes, I'm always true to you, darlin',
  in my way.

I enjoy a tender pass
By the boss of Boston, Mass.
Through his pass is middle class,
And not "Back Bay!"
But I'm always true to you, darlin',
  in my fashion,
Yes, I'm always true to you, darlin',
  in my way.

There's a madman known as "Mack"
Who is planning to attack.
If his mad attack means a Cadillac,
Okay!

But I'm always true to you, darlin',
  in my fashion,
Yes, I'm always true to you, darlin',
  in my way.

I've been asked to have a meal
By a big tycoon in steel.
If the meal includes a deal,
Accept I may!
But I'm always true to you, darlin',
  in my fashion,
Yes, I'm always true to you, darlin',
  in my way.

I could never curl my lip
To a dazzlin' diamond clip,
Though the clip meant "let 'er rip,"
I'd not say "Nay!"
But I'm always true to you, darlin',
  in my fashion,
Yes, I'm always true to you, darlin',
  in my way.

There's an oil man known as "Tex"
Who is keen to give me checks,
And his checks I fear,
Mean that Tex is here to stay!
But I'm always true to you, darlin',
  in my fashion,
Yes, I'm always true to you, darlin',
  in my way.

And All That Jazz

Words by Fred Ebb
Music by John Kander

from *Chicago*

Come on, babe, why don't we paint the town,
And all that jazz!
I'm gonna rouge my knees and roll my
   stockings down,
And all that jazz!
Start the car, I know a whoopee spot,
Where the gin is cold but the piano's hot.
It's just a noisy hall where there's a nightly
   brawl,
And all that jazz!

Slick your hair and wear your buckle shoes,
And all that jazz!
I hear that Father Dip is gonna blow the
   blues,
And all that jazz!
Hold on, hon, we're gonna bunny hug,
I bought some aspirin down at United Drug,
In case we shake apart and want a brand
   new start
To do that jazz!

Oh, I'm gonna see my Sheba shimmy shake.
(And all that jazz!)
Oh, she's gonna shimmy till her garters
   break.
(And all that jazz!)
Show her where to park her girdle,
Oh, her mother's blood'd curdle
If she'd hear her baby's queer
For all that jazz!

Voice 1:
Find a flask, we're playing fast and loose,
And all that jazz!
Right up here is where I store the juice,
And all that jazz!
Come on babe, we're gonna brush the sky.
I betcha Lucky Lindy never flew so high,
'Cause in the stratosphere, how could he
   lend an ear
To all that jazz!

Voice 2:
Oh, you're gonna see your Sheba shimmy
   shake,
And all that jazz!
Oh, I'm gonna shimmy till my garters break,
And all that jazz!
Show me where to park my girdle,
Oh, my mother's blood'd curdle,
If she'd hear her baby's queer
For all that jazz!

No, I'm no-one's wife,
But, oh, I love my life,
And all that jazz!
(Spoken) That jazz!

Another Hundred People

Music and Lyrics by Stephen Sondheim

from *Company*

Another hundred people just got off the train
And came up through the ground,
While another hundred people just got off the bus
And are looking around,
At another hundred people who got off of the plane
And are looking at us,
Who got off of the train
And the plane and the bus,
Maybe yesterday.

It's a city of strangers.
Some come to work, some to play.
A city of strangers,
Some come to stare, some to stay.
And ev'ry day,
The ones who stay,

Can find each other in the crowded streets
And the guarded parks,
By the rusty fountains and the dusty trees
With the battered barks,
And they walk together past the postered walls
With the crude remarks.

And they meet at parties through the friends of friends
Who they never know.
Will you pick me up or do I meet you there
Or shall we let it go?

Did you get my message 'cause I looked in vain?
Can we see each other Tuesday if it doesn't rain?
Look, I'll call you in the morning or my service will explain.
And another hundred people just got off the train.

Any Dream Will Do

Music by Andrew Lloyd Webber
Lyrics by Tim Rice

from *Joseph and the Amazing Technicolor® Dreamcoat*

I closed my eyes,
Drew back the curtain,
To see for certain
What I thought I knew.
Far, far away,
Someone was weeping,
But the world was sleeping.
Any dream will do.

I wore my coat,
With golden lining,
Bright colours shining,
Wonderful and new.
And in the east,
The dawn was breaking,
And the world was waking.
Any dream will do.

A crash of drums,
A flash of light,
My golden coat
Flew out of sight.
The colours faded into darkness,
I was left alone.

May I return,
To the beginning?
The light is dimming,
And the dream is too.
The world and I,
We are still waiting,
Still hesitating.
Any dream will do.

Any Place I Hang My Hat Is Home

Words by Johnny Mercer
Music by Harold Arlen

from *St. Louis Woman*

Free an' easy, that's my style,
Howdy do me, watch me smile,
Fare thee well me afterwhile,
'Cause I gotta roam.
An' any place I hang my hat is home!

Sweetnin' water, cherry wine,
Thank you kindly, suits me fine.
Kansas City, Caroline,
That's my honeycomb.
'Cause any place I hang my hat is home.

Birds roostin' in the tree pick up an' go,
An' the goin' proves
That's how it ought to be.
I pick up too,
When the spirit moves me.

Cross the river round the bend,
Howdy stranger, so long friend,
There's a voice in the lonesome win'
That keeps whisperin' roam!
I'm goin' where a welcome mat is,
No matter where that is,
'Cause any place I hang my hat is home.

As Long as He Needs Me

Words and Music by Lionel Bart

from *Oliver!*

As long as he needs me
Oh yes he does need me
In spite of what you see
I'm sure that he needs me

Who else would love him still
When they've been used so ill
He knows I always will
As long as he needs me.

I miss him so much
When he is gone
But when he's near me
I don't let on

The way I feel inside
The love I have to hide
The hell! I've got my pride
As long as he needs me

He doesn't say the things he should
He acts the way he thinks he should
But all the same I'll play
This game his way

As long as he needs me
I know where I must be
I'll cling on steadfastly
As long as he needs me

As long as life is long
I'll love him right or wrong
And somehow I'll be strong
As long as he needs me

If you are lonely
Then you will know
When someone needs you
You love them so

I won't betray his trust
Though people say I must
I've got to stay true
Just as long as he needs me

At the End of the Day

Music by Claude-Michel Schönberg
Lyrics by Herbert Kretzmer
Original Text by Alain Boublil and Jean-Marc Natel

from *Les Misérables*

At the end of the day you're another day
 older.
And that's all you can say for the life of the
 poor.
It's a struggle, it's a war.
And there's nothing that anyone's giving.
One more day standing about,
What is it for?
One less day to be living.

At the end of the day you're another day
 colder.
And the shirt on your back doesn't keep out
 the chill.
And the righteous hurry past,
They don't hear the little ones crying.
And the winter is coming on fast, ready to
 kill.
One day nearer to dying.

At the end of the day there's another day
 dawning.
And the sun in the morning is waiting to rise.
Like the waves crash on the sand,
Like a storm that'll break any second,
There's a hunger in the land.
There's a reckoning still to be reckoned.
And there's gonna be hell to pay
At the end of the day.

At the end of the day you get nothing for
 nothing.
Sitting flat on your butt doesn't buy any
 bread.
There are children back at home.
And the children have got to be fed.
And you're lucky to be in a job, and in a
 bed.
And we're counting our blessings.

At the end of the day, it's another day over,
With enough in your pocket to last for a
 week.
Pay the landlord, pay the shop.
Keep on grafting as long as you're able.
Keep on grafting till you drop,
Or it's back to the crumbs off the table.
Well, you've got to pay your way,
At the end of the day.

Autumn in New York

Words and Music by Vernon Duke

from *Thumbs Up*

It's time to end my lovely holiday
And bid the country a hasty farewell.
So on this gray and melancholy day
I'll move to a Manhattan hotel.
I'll dispose of my rose-colored chattels
And prepare for my share of adventures and
    battles.
Here on the twenty-seventh floor,
Looking down on the city I hate and adore!

Autumn in New York,
Why does it seem so inviting?
Autumn in New York,
It spells the thrill of first knighting.
Glimmering crowds and shimmering clouds
In canyons of steel,
They're making me feel I'm home.
It's autumn in New York,
That brings the promise of new love;
Autumn in New York
Is often mingled with pain.
Dreamers with empty hands
May sigh for exotic lands;
It's autumn in New York,
It's good to be alive again.

Autumn in New York,
The gleaming rooftops at sundown.
Autumn in New York,
It lifts you up when you're run down.
Jaded roués and gay divorcees
Who lunch at the Ritz,
Will tell you that "it's divine!"
This autumn in New York,
Transforms slums into Mayfair.
Autumn in New York,
You'll need no castles in Spain.
Lovers that bless the dark
On benches in Central Park
Greet autumn in New York;
It's good to be alive again.

Bali Ha'i

Lyrics by Oscar Hammerstein II
Music by Richard Rodgers

from *South Pacific*

Most people live on a lonely island,
Lost in the middle of a foggy sea.
Most people long for another island,
One where they know they would like to be.

Bali Ha'i
May call you,
Any night
Any day.
In your heart
You'll hear it call you:
"Come away,
Come away."

Bali Ha'i
Will whisper
On the wind
Of the sea:
"Here am I,
Your special island!
Come to me,
Come to me!"

Your own special hopes,
Your own special dreams,
Bloom on the hillside
And shine in the stream.

If you try,
You'll find me
Where the sky
Meets the sea;

"Here I am,
Your special island!
Come to me,
Come to me!"
Bali Ha'i
Bali Ha'i
Bali Ha'i.

Someday you'll see me,
Floating in the sunshine,
My head sticking out
From a low-flying cloud;
You'll hear me call you,
Singing through the sunshine,
Sweet and clear as can be:
"Come to me,
Here I am,
Come to me!"

Bali Ha'i
Will whisper
On the wind
Of the sea:
"Here am I,
Your special island!
Come to me,
Come to me."

Bali Ha'i
Bali Ha'i
Bali Ha'i.

Baubles, Bangles and Beads

Words and Music by Robert Wright and George Forrest
(Music Based on Themes of A. Borodin)

from *Kismet*

Baubles, bangles,
Hear how they jing-jing-a-ling-a,
Baubles, bangles,
Bright, shiny beads.
Sparkles, spangles,
My heart will sing, sing-a-ling-a,
Wearing baubles, bangles and beads.

I'll glitter and gleam so,
Make somebody dream so
That someday he may
Buy me a ring, ring-a-ling-a,
I've heard that's where it leads,
Wearing baubles, bangles and beads.

Barcelona

Music and Lyrics by Stephen Sondheim

from *Company*

Robert: Where you going?
April: Barcelona.
Robert: Oh—
April: Don't get up.
Robert: Do you have to?
April: Yes, I have to.
Robert: Oh—
April: Don't get up. Now you're angry.
Robert: No, I'm not.
April: Yes, you are.
Robert: No, I'm not. Put your things down.
April: See, you're angry.
Robert: No, I'm not.
April: Yes, you are.
Robert: No, I'm not. Put your wings down
   and stay.
April: I'm leaving.
Robert: Why?
April: To go to—
Robert: Stay.
April: I have to—
Both: Fly.
Robert: I know,
Both: To Barcelona.

Robert:
Look, you're a very special girl,
Not just overnight.
No, you're a very special girl,
And not because you're bright.
Not just because you're bright.
You're just a very special girl, June.

April: April.
Robert: April.
April: Thank you.

Robert: Whatcha thinking?
April: Barcelona.
Robert: Oh—
April: Flight eighteen.
Robert: Stay a minute.
April: I would like to.
Robert: So?
April: Don't be mean.
Robert: Stay a minute.
April: No, I can't.
Robert: Yes, you can.
April: No, I can't.
Robert: Where you going?
April: Barcelona.
Robert: So you said.
April: And Madrid—
Robert: Bon voyage—
April: On a Boeing.
Robert: Good night.
April: You're angry.
Robert: No.
April: I've go to—
Robert: Right.
April: Report to—
Robert: Go.

April:
That's not to say
That if I had my way,
Oh, well, I guess, okay.

Robert: What?
April: I'll stay.
Robert: But...Oh, God!

Beauty and the Beast

Lyrics by Howard Ashman
Music by Alan Menken

from Walt Disney's *Beauty and the Beast: The Broadway Musical*

Tale as old as time,
True as it can be.
Barely even friends,
Then somebody bends
Unexpectedly.

Just a little change.
Small, to say the least.
Both a little scared,
Neither one prepared.
Beauty and the Beast.
Ever just the same.
Ever a surprise.
Ever as before,
Ever just as sure
As the sun will rise.

Tale as old as time.
Tune as old as song.
Bittersweet and strange,
Finding you can change,
Learning you were wrong.

Certain as the sun
Rising in the East.
Tale as old as time,
Song as old as rhyme.
Beauty and the Beast.

Tale as old as time,
Song as old as rhyme
Beauty and the Beast.

Before the Parade Passes By

Music and Lyric by Jerry Herman

from *Hello, Dolly!*

Dolly:
Before the parade passes by,
I'm gonna get in step while there's still time left.
Before the parade passes by…

Before the parade passes by,
I'm gonna go and taste Saturday's high life.
Before the parade passes by,
I'm gonna get some life back into my life.
I'm ready to move out in front.
I've had enough of just passing by life.
With the rest of them,
With the best of them,
I can hold my head up high!
For I've got a goal again,
I've got a drive again,
I'm gonna feel my heart coming alive again,
Before the parade passes by.

Look at that crowd up ahead,
Listen and hear that brass harmony growing.
Look at that crowd up ahead,
Pardon me if my old spirit is showing.
All of those lights over there
Seem to be telling me where I'm going.
When the whistles blow,
And the cymbals crash,
And the sparklers light the sky,
I'm gonna raise the roof,
I'm gonna carry on,
Give me an old trombone,
Give me an old baton,
Before the parade passes by.

Chorus:
When the parade passes by,
Listen and hear that brass harmony
    growing.
When the parade passes by,
Pardon me if my old spirit is showing.
All of those lights over there
Seem to be telling me where I'm going.
When the whistles blow,
And the cymbals crash,
And the sparklers light the sky,
I'm gonna raise the roof,
I'm gonna carry on,
Give me an old trombone,
Give me an old baton.
Before the parade passes by.

I'm gonna raise the roof,
I'm gonna carry on,
Give me an old trombone,
Give me an old baton.
Before the parade passes by.

Being Alive

Music and Lyrics by Stephen Sondheim

from *Company*

Someone to hold you too close,
Someone to hurt you too deep,
Someone to sit in your chair
To ruin your sleep,
To make you aware
Of being alive,
Being alive.

Someone to need you too much,
Someone to know you too well,
Someone to pull you up short,
To put you through hell,
And give you support
Is being alive,
Being alive.

Someone you have to let in,
Someone whose feelings you spare,
Someone who, like it or not,
Will want you to share
A little, a lot,
Is being alive,
Being alive.

Someone to crowd you with love,
Someone to force you to care,
Someone to make you come through,
Who'll always be there
As frightened as you
Of being alive,
Being alive,
Being alive,
Being alive.

Somebody hold me too close,
Somebody hurt me too deep,
Somebody sit in my chair,
And ruin my sleep,
And make me aware
Of being alive.
Being alive.

Somebody need me too much,
Somebody know me too well,
Somebody pull me up short
And put me through hell,
And give me support
For being alive.
Being alive.
Make me alive.
Make me alive.
Make me confused,
Mock me with praise.
Let me be used,
Vary my days.
But alone is alone, not alive.

Somebody crowd me with love,
Somebody force me to care.
Somebody make me come through,
I'll always be here
As frightened as you,
To help us survive,
Being alive,
Being alive,
Being alive.

The Blue Room

Words by Lorenz Hart
Music by Richard Rodgers

from *The Girl Friend*

All my future plans,
Dear, will not suit your plans.
Read the little blueprints.
Here's your mother's room.
Here's your brother's room.
On the wall are two prints.
Here's the kiddie's room,
Here's the biddy's room,
Here's a pantry lined with shelves, dear.
Here I've planned for us
Something grand for us,
Where we two can be ourselves, dear.

Refrain:
We'll have a blue room,
A new room,
For two room,
Where every day's a holiday,
Because you're married to me.
Not like a ballroom,
A small room,
A hall room,
Where I can smoke my pipe away
With your wee head upon my knee.
We will thrive on,
Keep alive on,
Just nothing but kisses,
With Mister and Missus
On little blue chairs.

You sew your trousseau,
And Robinson Crusoe
Is not so far from worldly cares
As our blue room far away upstairs.

From all visitors
And inquisitors
We'll keep our apartment.
I won't change your plans—
You arrange your plans
Just the way your heart meant.
Here we'll be ourselves
And we'll see ourselves
Doing all the things we're scheming.
Here's a certain place,
Cretonne curtain place,
Where no one can see us dreaming.

Refrain

Bewitched

Words by Lorenz Hart
Music by Richard Rodgers

from *Pal Joey*

Note: There are two versions of the song's lyric, an original show version, and Hart's "standard version." Both are presented here.

SHOW LYRIC

After one whole quart of brandy,
Like a daisy I awake.
With no Bromo Selzer handy,
I don't even shake.
Men are not a new sensation;
I've done pretty well I think.
But this half-pint imitation
Put me on the blink.

Refrain 1:
I'm wild again, beguiled again,
A simpering, whimpering child again,
Bewitched, bothered and bewildered am I.
Couldn't sleep and wouldn't sleep
Until I could sleep where I shouldn't sleep,
Bewitched, bothered and bewildered am I.
Lost my heart, but what of it?
My mistake, I agree.
He's a laugh, but I love it
Because the laugh's on me.
A pill he is but still he is
All mine and I'll keep him until he is,
Bewitched, bothered and bewildered
    like me.

Refrain 2:
Seen a lot, I mean a lot
But now I'm like sweet sixteen a lot.
Bewitched, bothered and bewildered am I.
I'll sing to him, each spring to him,
And worship the trousers that cling to him.
Bewitched, bothered and bewildered am I.
When he talks, he is seeking
Words to get off his chest.
Horizontally speaking
He's at his very best.
Vexed again, perplexed again,
Thank God I can be oversexed again,
Bewitched, bothered and bewildered am I.

Refrain 3:
Sweet again, petite again,
And on my proverbial seat again,
Bewitched, bothered and bewildered am I.
What am I? Half shot am I.
To think that he loves me so hot am I,
Bewitched, bothered and bewildered am I.
Though at first we said, "No sir,"
Now we're two little dears.
You might say we are closer
Than Roebuck is to Sears.
I'm dumb again and numb again,
A rich, ready ripe little plumb again,
Bewitched, bothered and bewildered am I.

Reprise:
Wise at last, my eyes at last
Are cutting you down to your size at last,
Bewitched, bothered and bewildered
   no more.
Burned a lot, but learned a lot,
And now you are broke, though you
   earned a lot,
Bewitched, bothered and bewildered
   no more.
Couldn't eat, was dyspeptic,
Life was so hard to bear;
Now my heart's antiseptic,
Since you moved out of there.
Romance—finis; your chance—finis;
Those ants that invaded my pants—finis,
Bewitched, bothered and bewildered
   no more.

STANDARD LYRIC

Verse:
He's a fool and don't I know it,
But a fool can have his charms.
I'm in love and don't I show it
Like a babe in arms.
Love's the same old sad sensation,
Lately I've not slept a wink
Since this half-pint imitation
Put me on the blink.

Refrain:
I'm wild again, beguiled again,
A simpering, whimpering child again,
Bewitched, bothered and bewildered am I.
Couldn't sleep and wouldn't sleep
When love came and told me I shouldn't
   sleep,
Bewitched, bothered and bewildered am I.
Lost my heart, but what of it?
He is cold, I agree.
He's a laugh, but I love it
Although the laugh's on me.
I'll sing to him, each spring to him,
And long for the day when I cling to him,
Bewitched, bothered and bewildered am I.

Bosom Buddies

Music and Lyric by Jerry Herman

from *Mame*

Mame and Vera:
We'll always be bosom buddies,
Friends, sisters and pals.
We'll always be bosom buddies.
If life should reject you,
There's me to protect you.
Vera:
If I say that your tongue is vicious,
Mame:
If I call you uncouth,
Both:
It's simply that,
Who else but a bosom buddy
Will sit down and tell you the truth?

Vera (Spoken):
Though now and again I'm aware
That my candid opinion may sting,
Mame (Spoken):
Though often my frank observation might
    scald,
I've been meaning to tell you for years
You should keep your hair nat'ral, like mine.
Vera (Spoken):
If I kept my hair nat'ral like yours, I'd be
    bald!
(Sung) But, darling,

Both:
We'll always be dear companions.
Vera:
My crony.
Mame:
My mate.
Both:
We'll always be harmonizing,
Vera:
Orphan Annie and Sandy,
Both:
Like Amos and Andy.

Vera:
If I say that your sense of style's
As far off as your youth,
It's only that,
Who else but a bosom buddy
Will tell you the whole stinkin' truth?

Mame (Spoken):
Each time that a critic has written:
"Your voice is the voice of a frog,"
Straight to your side to defend you, I rush.
You know that I'm there
Ev'ry time that the world
Makes an unkind remark.
When they say:
"Vera Charles is the world's greatest lush,"
(Sung) It hurts me.

Vera:
And if I say your fangs are showing,
Mame, pull in your claws,
It's simply that,
Who else but a bosom buddy
Would notice the obvious flaws.

Mame (Spoken):
I feel it's my duty to tell you it's time
To adjust your age.
You try to be "Peg O' My Heart,"
When you're Lady Macbeth!
Exactly how old are you, Vera?
The truth!
Vera (Spoken):
Well, how old do you think?
Mame (Spoken):
I'd say somewhere in between forty and
    death!

Both:
But sweetie,
Vera:
I'll always be Alice Toklas,
If you'll be Gertrude Stein.
And tho' I'll admit I've dished you,
I've gossiped and gloated,
But I'm so devoted.

Mame (Spoken):
And if I say that sex and guts
(Sung) Made you into a star,
Remember that,
Who else but a bosom buddy
Will tell you how rotten you are?

Both:
Just turn to your bosom buddy
For aid and affection,
For help and direction,
For loyalty, love and forsooth,
Remember that,
Who else but a bosom buddy
Will sit down and level,
And give you the devil,
Will sit down and tell you the truth?!

Breeze off the River

Words and Music by David Yazbek

from *The Full Monty*

There's a breeze off the river,
Through the crack in the window pane.
There's my boy on the pillow,
And I feel like I'm lost again.

Ev'rybody knows the secret.
They all know what their life should be,
And they move like a river.
Ev'rybody knows except for me.

And I never feel like somebody,
Somebody calls a father,
I can't explain.
But when I look at you, kid,
It's like a mirror.
It spins my head.
It wakes me.

Like the breeze off the river,
Ev'ry time I see your face.
And it's strange but familiar,
Like a map of a better place.

And sometimes I feel like I live in a shadow,
And shadow's all I see.
Then you jump straight up,
And you grab the moon,
And you make it shine on me.
Where do you get it from?

Ev'rybody knows the secret.
Well I don't and I never did.
I don't know any secret.
All I know is I love you, kid.

Broadway Baby

Words and Music by Stephen Sondheim

from *Follies*

I'm just a Broadway Baby,
Walking off my tired feet,
Pounding Forty Second Street
To be in a show.

Broadway Baby,
Learning how to sing and dance,
Waiting for that one big chance
To be in a show.

Gee, I'd like to be
On some marquee,
All twinkling lights,
A spark to pierce the dark
From Batt'ry Park
To Washington Heights.

Some day maybe,
All my dreams will be repaid.
Heck I'd even play the maid
To be in a show.

Say, Mister producer,
Some girls get the breaks.
Just give me my cue, sir,
I've got what it takes.
Say, Mister producer
I'm talkin' to you sir.
I don't need a lot,
Only what I got,
Plus a tube of greasepaint
And a follow spot!

I'm a Broadway Baby,
Slaving at the five and ten,
Dreaming of the great day when
I'll be in a show.
Broadway Baby,
Making rounds all afternoon,
Eating at a greasy spoon
To save on my dough.

At my tiny flat
There's just my cat,
A bed and a chair.
Still I'll stick it till
I'm on a bill
All over Times Square.

Some day maybe,
If I stick it long enough,
I can get to strut my stuff,
Working for a nice man,
Like a Ziegfeld or a Weissman,
In a big-time Broadway show!

Brush Up Your Shakespeare

Words and Music by Cole Porter

from *Kiss Me, Kate*

The girls today in society
Go for classical poetry,
So, to win their hearts,
One must quote with ease
Aeschylus and Euripides.
One must know Homer and b'lieve me, bo,
Sophocles, also Sapphoho,
Unless you know Shelley and Keats and Pope,
Dainty debbies will call you a dope.
But the poet of them all,
Who will start 'em simply ravin'
Is the poet people call
The bard of Stratford-on-Avon.

Brush up your Shakespeare,
Start quoting him now.
Brush up your Shakespeare
And the women you will wow.
Just declaim a few lines from "Othella"
And they'll think you're a heck-uv-a fella,
If your blonde won't respond when you flat-
ter 'er
Tell her what Tony told Cleopatterer.
And if still to be shocked she pretends, well,
Just remind her that "All's Well That
End's Well."
Brush up your Shakespeare
And they'll all kow-tow.

Brush up your Shakespeare,
Start quoting him now.
Brush up your Shakespeare
And the women you will wow.
If your goil is a Washington Heights dream,
Treat the kid to "A Midsummer Night's
Dream,"
With the wife of the British embessida
Try a crack out of "Troilus and Cressida."
If she says she won't buy it or tike* it,
Make her tike it, what's more,
"As You Like It."
Brush up your Shakespeare
And they'll all kow-tow.

Brush up your Shakespeare,
Start quoting him now.
Brush up your Shakespeare
And the women you will wow.
If you can't be a ham and do "Hamlet"
They will not give a damn or a damnlet.
Just recite an occasional sonnet,
And your lap'll have Honey upon it.
When your baby is pleading for pleasure
Let her sample your "Measure for Measure."
Brush up your Shakespeare
And they'll all kow-tow.

*Cockney for "take"

By Myself

Words by Howard Dietz
Music by Arthur Schwartz

from *Between the Devil*

I'll go by myself.
This is the end of romance.
I'll go my way by myself.
Love is only a dance.

I'll try to apply myself,
And teach my heart how to sing.
I'll go my way by myself,
Like a bird on the wing.

I'll face the unknown,
I'll build a world of my own;
No one knows better than I myself,
I'm by myself, alone.

But in the Morning, No

Words and Music by Cole Porter

from *DuBarry Was a Lady*

He:
Love affairs among gentility
Hit the rocks with great agility,
Either because of income
Or incompatibility.

She:
We've adjusted our finances,
You run mine and I run France's,
So there's only one question that's hot,
Will we have fun or not?

Refrain
She:
Are you fond of riding, dear?
Kindly tell me, if so.
He:
Yes, I'm fond of riding, dear,
But in the morning, no!
She:
Are you good at shooting, dear?
Kindly tell me, if so.
He:
Yes, I'm good at shooting, dear,
But in the morning, no!
When the dawn's early light
Comes to crucify my night,
That's the time
When I'm in low.
She:
Are you fond of boxing, dear?
Kindly tell me, if so.

He:
Yes, I'm fond of boxing, dear,
But in the morning, no, no—no, no,
No, no, no, no, no!

ADDITIONAL LYRICS
Refrain 2
He:
Do you like the mountains, dear?
Kindly tell me, if so.
She:
Yes, I like the mountains, dear,
But in the morning, no!
He:
Are you good at climbing, dear?
Kindly tell me, if so.
She:
Yes, I'm good at climbing, dear,
But in the morning, no!
When the light of day
Comes and drags me from the hay,
That's the time
When I'm in low.
He:
Have you tried Pike's Peak, my dear?
Kindly tell me, if so.
She:
Yes, I've tried Pike's Peak, my dear,
But in the morning, no, no—no, no,
No, no, no, no, no!

Refrain 3
She:
Are you fond of swimming, dear?
Kindly tell me, if so.
He:
Yes, I'm fond of swimming, dear,
But in the morning, no!
She:
Can you do the crawl, my dear?
Kindly tell me, if so.
He:
I can do the crawl, my dear,
But in the morning, no.
When the sun through the blind
Starts to burn my poor behind,
That's the time
When I'm in low.
She:
Do you use the breast stroke, dear?
Kindly tell me, if so.
He:
Yes, I use the breast stroke, dear,
But in the morning, no, no—no, no,
No, no, no, no, no!

Refrain 4
He:
Are you fond of Hot Springs, dear?
Kindly tell me, if so.
She:
Yes, I'm fond of Hot Springs, dear,
But in the morning, no!

He:
D'you like old Point Comfort, dear?
Kindly tell me, if so.
She:
I like old Point Comfort, dear,
But in the morning, no.
When my maid toddles in
With my orange juice and gin,
That's the time
When I'm in low.
He:
Do you like Miami, dear?
Kindly tell me, if so.
She:
Yes, I like your-ami, dear,
But in the morning, no, no—no, no,
No, no, no, no, no!

Refrain 5
She:
Are you good at football, dear?
Kindly tell me, if so.
He:
Yes, I'm good at football, dear,
But in the morning, no!
She:
Do you ever fumble, dear?
Kindly tell me, if so.
He:
No, I never fumble, dear,
But in the morning, yes.
When I start with a frown,

(continues)

("But in the Morning, No", *continued*)

Reading Winchell upside down,
That's the time
When I'm in low.
She:
Do you like to scrimmage, dear?
Kindly tell me, if so.
He:
Yes, I like a scrimmage, dear,
But in the morning, no, no—no, no,
No, no, no, no, no!

Refrain 6
He:
D'you like Nelson Eddy, dear?
Kindly tell me, if so.
She:
I like Nelson Eddy, dear,
But in the morning, no!
He:
D'you like Tommy Manville, dear?
Kindly tell me, if so.
She:
I like Tommy Manville, dear,
But in the morning, no.
When my maid says, "Madame!
Wake 'em up and make 'em scram,"
That's the time
When I'm in low.
He:
Are you fond of Harvard men?
Kindly tell me, if so.

She:
Yes, I'm fond of Harvard men,
But in the morning, no, no—no, no,
No, no, no, no, no!

Refrain 7
She:
Are you good at figures, dear?
Kindly tell me, if so.
He:
Yes, I'm good at figures, dear,
But in the morning, no.
She:
D'you do double entry, dear?
Kindly tell me, if so.
He:
I do double entry, dear,
But in the morning, no.
When the sun on the rise,
Shows the bags beneath my eyes,
That's the time
When I'm in low.
She:
Are you fond of business, dear?
Kindly tell me, if so.
He:
Yes, I'm fond of business, dear,
But in the morning, no, no—no, no,
No, no, no, no, no!

Refrain 8
He:
Are you in the market, dear?
Kindly tell me, if so.

She:
Yes, I'm in the market, dear,
But in the morning, no!
He:
Are you fond of bulls and bears?
Kindly tell me, if so.
She:
Yes, I'm fond of bulls and bears,
But in the morning, no.
When I'm waked by my fat
Old canary, singing flat,
That's the time
When I'm in low.
He:
Would you ever sell your seat?
Kindly tell me, if so.
She:
Yes, I'd gladly sell my seat,
But in the morning, no, no—no, no,
No, no, no, no, no!

Refrain 9
She:
Are you fond of poker, dear?
Kindly tell me, if so.
He:
Yes, I'm fond of poker, dear,
But in the morning, no!
She:
Do you ante up, my dear?
Kindly tell me, if so.
He:
Yes, I ante up, my dear,
But in the morning, no.
When my old Gunga Din,

Brings the Bromo Seltzer in,
That's the time
When I'm in low.
She:
Can you fill an inside straight?
Kindly tell me, if so.
He:
I've filled plenty inside straight,
But in the morning, no, no—no, no,
No, no, no, no, no!

Refrain 10
He:
Are you fond of Democrats?
Kindly tell me, if so.
She:
Yes, I'm fond of Democrats,
But in the morning, no!
He:
Do you like Republicans?
Kindly tell me, if so.
She:
Yes, I like Republicans,
But in the morning, no.
When my pet pekinese
Starts to cross his Q's and P's,
That's the time
When I'm in low.
He:
Do you like third parties, dear?
Kindly tell me, if so.
She:
Yes, I love third parties, dear,
But in the morning, no, no—no, no,
No, no, no, no, no!

Bye Bye Baby

Words by Leo Robin
Music by Jule Styne

from *Gentlemen Prefer Blondes*

I'll be in my room alone
Ev'ry Post Meridian,
And I'll be with my diary
And that book by Mister Gideon.

Refrain:
Bye bye baby!
Remember you're my baby
When they give you the eye.
Although I know that you care,
Won't you write and declare
That though on the loose,
You are still on the square.

I'll be gloomy,
But send that rainbow to me,
Then my shadows will fly,
Though you'll be gone for awhile,
I know that I'll be smiling
With my baby, bye and bye.

Refrain

With my baby, bye and bye.

C'est Magnifique

Words and Music by Cole Porter

from *Can-Can*

Love is such a fantastic affair,
When it comes to call,
After taking you up in the air,
Down it lets you fall.
But be patient and soon you will find,
If you follow your heart, not your mind,
Love is waiting there, again,
To take you up in the air, again.

Refrain:
When love comes in,
And takes you for a spin,
Oo-la-la-la,
C'est magnifique.
When ev'ry night
Your loved one holds you tight,
Oo-la-la-la,
C'est magnifique.
But when, one day,
Your loved one drifts away,
Oo-la-la-la,
It is so tragique.
But when, once more,
He [She] whispers,
"Je t'adore,"
C'est magnifique.

Refrain

ADDITIONAL LYRICS
Verse 2:
When you began of love to speak,
I followed every word.
But when you called love magnifique,
I would have called it absurd.
And when you said it was often tragique,
I would have said it was always comique.
So, mad'moiselle, be sweet to me,
And kindly do not repeat to me.

Cabaret

Words by Fred Ebb
Music by John Kander

from the Musical *Cabaret*

What good is sitting alone in your room?
Come hear the music play;
Life is a cabaret, old chum,
Come to the cabaret.

Put down your knitting, the book and the
    broom,
Time for a holiday;
Life is a cabaret, old chum,
Come to the cabaret.

Come taste the wine,
Come hear the band.
Come blow the horn, start celebrating,
Right this way your table's waiting.

No use permitting some prophet of doom,
To wipe every smile away;
Life is a cabaret, old chum.
Come to the cabaret.

I used to have a girlfriend known as Elsie,
With whom I shared four sordid rooms in
    Chelsea.
She wasn't what you'd call a blushing flower,
As a matter of fact she rented by the hour.
The day she died the neighbors came to
    snicker:
"Well, that's what comes of too much pills
    and liquor."

But when I saw her laid out like a queen,
She was the happiest corpse I'd ever seen.
I think of Elsie to this very day.
I remember how she'd turn to me and say:

What good is sitting alone in your room?
Come hear the music play;
Life is a cabaret, old chum,
Come to the cabaret.

Put down your knitting, the book and the
    broom,
Time for a holiday;
Life is a cabaret, old chum,
Come to the cabaret.

And as for me, as for me,
I made my mind up back in Chelsea,
When I go I'm going like Elsie.

Start by admitting from cradle to tomb
Isn't that long a stay;
Life is a cabaret, old chum,
Only a cabaret, old chum
And I love a cabaret.

Can You Feel the Love Tonight

Music by Elton John
Lyrics by Tim Rice

from Disney Presents *The Lion King: The Broadway Musical*

There's a calm surrender
To the rush of the day,
When the heat of the rolling world
Can be turned away.
An enchanted moment,
And it sees me through.
It's enough for this restless warrior
Just to be with you.

Refrain:
And can you feel the love tonight?
It is where we are.
It's enough for this wide-eyed wanderer
That we got this far.
And can you feel the love tonight,
How it's laid to rest?
It's enough to make kings and vagabonds
Believe the very best.

There's a time for everyone,
If they only learn,
That the twisting kaleidoscope
Moves us all in turn.
There's a rhyme and reason
To the wild outdoors,
When the heart of this star-crossed voyager
Beats in time with yours.

Refrain

Castle on a Cloud

Music by Claude-Michel Schönberg
Lyrics by Herbert Kretzmer
Original Text by Alain Boublil and Jean-Marc Natel

from *Les Misérables*

There is a castle on a cloud.
I like to go there in my sleep.
Aren't any floors for me to sweep,
Not in my castle on a cloud.

There is a room that's full of toys.
There are a hundred boys and girls.
Nobody shouts or talks too loud,
Not in my castle on a cloud.

There is a lady all in white,
Holds me and sings a lullaby.
She's nice to see and she's soft to touch.
She says, "Cosette, I love you very much."

I know a place where no one's lost.
I know a place where no one cries.
Crying at all is not allowed,
Not in my castle on a cloud.

Circle of Life

Music by Elton John
Lyrics by Tim Rice

from Disney Presents *The Lion King: The Broadway Musical*

From the day we arrive on the planet
And blinking, step into the sun,
There's more to be seen than can ever be seen,
More to do than can ever be done.

Some say, "Eat or be eaten."
Some say, "Live and let live."
But all are agreed
As they join the stampede,
You should never take more than you give
In the circle of life.

Refrain:
It's the wheel of fortune.
It's the leap of faith.
It's the band of hope
Till we find our place
On the path unwinding
In the circle of life.

Some of us fall by the wayside,
And some of us soar to the stars.
And some of us sail through our troubles,
And some have to live with the scars.
There's far too much to take in here,
More to find than can ever be found.
But the sun rolling high
Through the sapphire sky
Keeps great and small on the endless round
In the circle of life.

Refrain Twice

On the path unwinding
In the circle,
The circle of life.

Class

Words by Fred Ebb
Music by John Kander

from *Chicago*

What ever happened to fair dealing,
And pure ethics and nice manners?
Why is it ev'ryone now is a pain in the ass?
What ever happened to class?
Class!

What ever happened to "please, may I?"
And "yes, thank you," and "how charming!"
Now ev'ry son of a bitch is a snake in the
grass.
What ever happened to class?
Class!

Ah, there ain't no gentlemen to open up the
doors,
There ain't no ladies now there's only pigs
and whores,
And even kids'll knock ya down so's they can
pass.
Nobody's got no class.

What ever happened to old values,
And fine morals, and good breeding?
Now no one even says "oops,"
When they're passing their gas.
What ever happened to class?
Class!

Ah, there ain't no gentlemen who's fit for any
use,
And any girl'd touch your privates for a
deuce.
And even kids'll kick your shins and give you
sass.
Nobody's got no class.

All you read about today is rape and theft.
Jesus Christ!
Ain't there no decency left?
Nobody's got no class.

Ev'rybody you watch
S'got his brains in his crotch.
Holy crap (holy crap),
What a shame (what a shame).
What's become of class?

Climb Ev'ry Mountain

Lyrics by Oscar Hammerstein II
Music by Richard Rodgers

from *The Sound of Music*

Climb every mountain,
Search high and low,
Follow every byway,
Every path you know.

Climb every mountain,
Ford every stream,
Follow every rainbow,
Till you find your dream!
A dream that will need all the love you can give,
Every day of your life for as long as you live.

Climb every mountain,
Ford every stream,
Follow every rainbow
Till you find your dream!

Come Along with Me

Words and Music by Cole Porter

from *Can-Can*

From down to up about this town,
I've drunk my cup from up to down,
But being a connoisseur and a great social pet,
The circle which I prefer is the dilettante set.
Come along, little lambkin, do,
Let me show it to you.

Refrain:
If you want to pass through the gilded gates,
Where the bourgeois meet the sophisticates
To exchange their views and to compare their mates,
Come along with me.

A princess from Rome I have lately met,
Who attracts the crowd that plays hard to get
By her dry chianti and her wet spaghett!
Come along with me.

Come along with me, my pretty,
Let me open your eyes,
In this great big wicked city
It is folly not to be wise.

And if any night, baby, you would care
For an intellectual love affair,
I'll improve your mind, if you let down your hair.
Come along, woof, woof,
Come along, woof, woof,
Come along with me.
(Spoken) Woof!

Refrain

Come Back to Me

Words by Alan Jay Lerner
Music by Burton Lane

from *On a Clear Day You Can See Forever*

Hear my voice where you are!
Take a train, steal a car,
Hop a freight, grab a star,
Come back to me!

Catch a plane, catch a breeze,
On your hands, on your knees,
Swim or fly, only please
Come back to me.

On a mule, in a jet,
With your hair in a net,
In a towel ringing wet,
I don't care,
This is where you should be.

From the hills, from the shore,
Ride the wind to my door.
Turn the highway to dust!
Break the law if you must!
Move the world, only just
Come back to me!

(Spoken) Blast your hide! Hear me call!
(Sung) Must I fight City Hall?
Here and now,
(Spoken) Damn it all,
(Sung) Come back to me!

What on earth must I do,
Scream and yell till I'm blue?
(Spoken) Curse your soul,
(Sung) When will you come back to me?

Have you gone to the moon,
Or the corner saloon,
And to rack and to "roon?"
Mad'moiselle, where the hell can you be?

In a crate, in a trunk,
On a horse, on a drunk,
In a Rolls or a van,
Wrapped in mink or Saran;
Any way that you can,
Come back to me!

Come Rain or Come Shine

Words by Johnny Mercer
Music by Harold Arlen

from *St. Louis Woman*

I'm gonna love you like nobody's loved you,
Come rain or come shine.
High as the mountain and deep as the river,
Come rain or come shine.
I guess when you met me
It was just one of those things,
But don't ever bet me
'Cause I'm gonna be true if you let me.

You're gonna love me like nobody's loved me,
Come rain or come shine.
Happy together, unhappy together and won't it be fine.
Days may be cloudy or sunny.
We're in or we're out of the money,
But I'm with you always
I'm with you rain or shine.

Comedy Tonight

Words and Music by Stephen Sondheim

from *A Funny Thing Happened on the Way to the Forum*

Something familiar, something peculiar,
Something for everyone, a comedy tonight!
Something appealing, something appalling.
Something for everyone, a comedy tonight!

Nothing with kings, nothing with crowns.
Bring on the lovers, liars and clowns!
Old situations, new complications,
Nothing portentous or polite;
Tragedy tomorrow, comedy tonight!

Something convulsive, something repulsive,
Something for everyone, a comedy tonight!
Something esthetic, something frenetic,
Something for everyone, a comedy tonight.

Nothing of Gods, nothing of Fate.
Weighty affairs will just have to wait.
Nothing that's formal, nothing that's normal,
No recitations to recite!
Open up the curtain, comedy tonight.

Diamonds Are a Girl's Best Friend

Words by Leo Robin
Music by Jule Styne

from *Gentlemen Prefer Blondes*

A kiss on the hand may be quite continental,
But diamonds are a girl's best friend.
A kiss may be grand but it won't pay the rental
On your humble flat,
Or help you at the Automat.
Men grow cold as girls grow old
And we all lose our charms in the end.
But square cut or pear-shape,
These rocks don't lose their shape,
Diamonds are a girl's best friend.

There may come a time when a lass needs a lawyer,
But diamonds are a girl's best friend.
There may come a time when a hard-boiled employer
Thinks you're awful nice,
But get that "ice" or else no dice.
He's your guy when stocks are high,
But beware when they start to descend.
It's then that those louses go back to their spouses,
Diamonds are a girl's best friend.

Disgustingly Rich

Words by Lorenz Hart
Music by Richard Rodgers

from *Higher and Higher*

Brenda Frazier sat on a wall,
Brenda Frazier had a big fall.
Brenda Frazier's falling down,
Falling down, falling down.
Brenda Frazier's falling down,
My fair Minnie!

There's money in the movies,
There's money in the ads.
There's money in the old Johns,
There's money in the lads.

Minnie, Minnie, Minnie, Minnie,
Money, Money, Money, Money,
Eeny, Meeny Money Mo.
Catch a fortune by the toe!

I'll buy ev'rything I wear at Sacks,
I'll cheat plenty on my income tax,
Swear like a trouper, live in a stupor,
Just disgustingly rich!

I'll make money and I'll make it quick,
Boosting cigarettes that make me sick.
Smothered in sables like Betty Grable's
Just disgustingly rich!

I will buy land
Down on Long Island,
And as a resident,
I will pan the President.
I'll aspire
Higher and higher.

I'll get married and adopt a son
Right from Tony's or from Twenty-One.
Swimming in highballs, stewed to the
    eyeballs,
Just disgustingly rich,
Too, too disgustingly rich!

Break my ankles on the tennis courts,
Get pneumonia doing winter sports.
I won't be civil, rude as the divil,
Just disgustingly rich!

Ev'ry weekend I will sail the sea
On my little yacht, the Normandie.
Catch barracuda down in Bermuda,
Just disgustingly rich!

I'll eat salmon.
I'll play backgammon.
Turn breakfast into lunch.
I'll take Errol Flynn to lunch.
I'll aspire
Higher and higher.

I'll buy autos like the autocrats.
I'll drink Pluto like the plutocrats.
Playing the horses, getting divorces.
Just disgustingly rich,
Too, too disgustingly rich!

Do I Hear a Waltz?

Music by Richard Rodgers
Lyrics by Stephen Sondheim

from *Do I Hear a Waltz?*

Do I hear a waltz?
Very odd, but I hear a waltz.
There isn't a band,
And I don't understand it at all.

I can't hear a waltz.
Oh my Lord, there it goes again!
Why is nobody dancing in the street?
Can't they hear the beat?

Refrain:
Magical, mystical miracle!
Can it be? Is it true?
Things are impossibly lyrical!
Is it me? No, it's you!

I do hear a waltz!
I see you and I hear a waltz!
It's what I've been waiting for.
An old lady is waltzing in her flat,
Waltzing with her cat!

Roses are dancing with peonies!
Yes, it's true! Can't you see?
Ev'rything's suddenly Viennese!
Can't be you! Must be me!

Do I hear a waltz?
I want more than to hear a waltz!
I want you to share it 'cause,
Oh, boy, do I hear a waltz?

Refrain

I hear a waltz!

Do I Love You Because You're Beautiful?

Lyrics by Oscar Hammerstein II
Music by Richard Rodgers

from *Cinderella*

Do I love you
Because you're beautiful,
Or are you beautiful
Because I love you?
Am I making believe I see you,
A girl too lovely to
Be really true?
Do I want you
Because you're wonderful?
Or are you wonderful
Because I want you?
Are you the sweet invention of a lover's dream?
Or are you really as beautiful as you seem?

Don't Rain on My Parade

Words by Bob Merrill
Music by Jule Styne

from *Funny Girl*

Don't tell me not to live,
Just sit and putter.
Life's candy and the sun's
A ball of butter.
Don't bring around a cloud
To rain on my parade!

Don't tell me not to fly,
I've simply got to.
If someone takes a spill,
It's me and not you.
Who told you you're allowed
To rain on my parade?

Refrain:
I'll march my band out,
I'll beat my drum.
And if I'm fanned out,
Your turn at bat, sir,
At least I didn't fake it.
Hat, sir!
I guess I didn't make it.

But whether I'm the rose
Of sheer perfection,
Or freckle on the nose
Of life's complexion,
The cinder or the shiny apple
Of its eye,

I gotta fly once,
I gotta try once,
Only can die once.
Right, sir?
Ooh, love is juicy,
Juicy and you see
I gotta have my bite, sir!

Get ready for me, love,
'Cause I'm a "comer."
I simply gotta march,
'Cause I'm a drummer.
Don't bring around a cloud
To rain on my parade.

I'm gonna live and live now!
Get what I want I know how.
One roll for the whole shebang!
One throw, that bell will go clang!
Eye on the target and wham!
One shot, one gun shot and bam!
Hey, Mister Arnstein,
Here I am!

Refrain

Get ready for me, love,
'Cause I'm a "comer."
I simply gotta march,
My heart's a drummer.
Nobody, no, nobody
Is gonna rain on my parade!

Easter Parade

Words and Music by Irving Berlin

from *As Thousands Cheer*

Never saw you look quite so pretty before.
Never saw you dressed quite so lovely, what's more.
I could hardly wait
To keep our date
This lovely Easter morning.
And my heart beat fast
As I came through the door for:

In your Easter bonnet,
With all the frills upon it,
You'll be the grandest lady
In the Easter Parade.

I'll be all in clover
And when they look you over
I'll be the proudest fellow
In the Easter Parade.

On the Avenue,
Fifth Avenue,
The photographers
Will snap us.
And you'll find that you're
In the rotogravure.

Oh, I could write a sonnet
About your Easter bonnet
And of the girl I'm taking to the Easter Parade.

Elaborate Lives

Music by Elton John
Lyrics by Tim Rice

from Walt Disney Theatrical Productions' *Aida*

Radames:
We all lead such elaborate lives,
Wild ambitions in our sights.
How an affair of the heart survives,
Days apart and hurried nights.
Seems quite unbelievable to me.
I don't want to live like that.
Seems quite unbelievable to me.
I don't want to love like that.
I just want our time to be
Slower and gentler,
Wiser, free.

We all live in extravagant times,
Playing games we can't all win.
Unintended emotional crimes.
Take some out, take others in.
I'm so tired of all we're going through.
I don't want to live like that.
I'm so tired of all we're going through.
I don't want to love like that.
I just want to be with you,
Now and forever,
Peaceful, true.

This may not be the moment
To tell you face to face,
But I could wait forever
For the perfect time and place.

Radames and Aida:
We all lead such elaborate lives.
We don't know whose words are true.
Strangers, lovers, husbands, wives,
Hard to know who's loving who.
Too many choices tear us apart.
I don't want to live like that.

Radames:
Too many choices
Tear us apart.
I don't want to love like that,
I just want to touch your heart.
May this confession
Both:
Be the start.

Everything's Coming Up Roses

Words by Stephen Sondheim
Music by Jule Styne

from *Gypsy*

I had a dream,
A dream about you, Baby!
It's gonna come true, Baby!
They think that we're through,
But Baby.

You'll be swell,
You'll be great,
Gonna have the whole world on a plate.
Starting here,
Starting now,
Honey, everything's coming up roses!

Clear the decks,
Clear the tracks,
You got nothing to do but relax,
Blow a kiss,
Take a bow,
Honey, everything's coming up roses!

Now's your inning,
Stand the world on its ear!
Set it spinning,
That'll be just the beginning!

Curtain up,
Light the lights,
You got nothing to hit but the heights!
You'll be swell,
You'll be great!
I can tell, just you wait!
That lucky star I talk about is due!
Honey, everything's coming up roses for me
    and for you!

You can do it,
All you need is a hand.
We can do it,
Momma is gonna see to it!

Curtain up!
Light the lights!
We got nothing to hit but the heights!
I can tell,
Wait and see,
There's the bell,
Follow me!
And nothing's gonna stop us till we're
    through!
Honey, everything's coming up roses and
    daffodils,
Everything's coming up sunshine and
    Santa Claus,
Everything's gonna be bright-lights and
    lollipops.
Everything's coming up roses for me and for
    you.

Exactly Like You

Words by Dorothy Fields
Music by Jimmy McHugh

from *International Revue*
featured in *Sugar Babies*

I know why I've waited, know why I've been blue,
Prayed each night for someone exactly like you.
Why should we spend money on a show or two.
No one does those love scenes exactly like you.

You make me feel so grand.
I want to hand the world to you.
You seem to understand,
Each foolish little scheme I'm scheming,
Dream I'm dreaming.
Now I know why mother taught me to be true.
She meant me for someone exactly like you.

Falling in Love with Love

Words by Lorenz Hart
Music by Richard Rodgers

from *The Boys from Syracuse*

I weave with brightly colored strings
To keep my mind off other things;
So, ladies, let your fingers dance,
And keep your hands out of romance.
Lovely witches,
Let the stitches
Keep your fingers under control.
Cut the thread, but leave
The whole heart whole.
Merry maids can sew and sleep;
Wives can only sew and weep!

Refrain:
Falling in love with love
Is falling for make-believe.
Falling in love with love
Is playing the fool.
Caring too much is such
A juvenile fancy.
Learning to trust is just
For children in school.
I fell in love with love
One night when the moon was full.
I was unwise, with eyes
Unable to see.
I fell in love with love,
With love everlasting,
But love fell out with me.

From Alpha to Omega

Words and Music by Cole Porter

from *You Never Know*

You're such a ne plus ultra creature,
That if I had your photo,
I couldn't pick my fav'rite feature,
I like you so in toto.
In ev'ry way, from ev'ry angle,
You're the bangle I long to dangle,
For from basement to roof,
From Wagner op'ra to op'ra bouffe,

Refrain:
From Alpha to Omega,
From A to Z,
From Alpha to Omega,
You're made for me.
From left hooks by Dempsey,
To Braddock's upper cuts,
From Jericho to Kokomo,
Not to mention from soup to nuts;
From *Journal* until *Mirror*,
From coast to coast,
From Juliet to Norma Shearer,
You're what I like the most.
And from morning until evening,
In mis'ry I shall pine,
'Til from Alpha to Omega, you're mine.

Refrain

ADDITIONAL LYRICS
Refrain 2:
From Alpha to Omega,
From A to Z,
From Alpha to Omega,
You're made for me.
From love songs by Schumann
To hits by Jerry Kern,
From Sarawak to Hackensack,
Not to mention, from stem to stern.
From dyah Missus Pat Campbell
To sweet Mae West,
You happen to be the mammal
This body loves the best,
And from morning until evening,
Will you stun yourself with wine?
Certainly, 'til from Alpha to Omega, you're
   mine.

Refrain 3:
From Alpha to Omega,
From A to Z,
From Alpha to Omega,
You're made for me.
From Lou Gehrig's home-run
To Lou Chiozza's bunt,
From Tripoli to Kankakee,
Not to mention from Lynn to Lunt,

THE LYRIC LIBRARY

From great eighty-pound codfish,
To sardines canned,
You happen to be the odd fish
This lad would love to land,
And will you woo me and pursue me,
With sinker, hook, and line?
Yes, till from Alpha to Omega you're mine.
And will you chase me,
And embrace me,
And say that I'm divine?
'Til from Alpha to Omega, you're mine.

Refrain 4:
From Alpha to Omega,
From A to Z,
From Alpha to Omega,
You're made for me.
From cotton ploughed under,
To this year's bumper crop,
From Benzedrine to Ovaltine,
Not to mention, from go to stop.
From corn muffins to Triscuit,
From fat to thin,
From Zev to the young Seabiscuit,
I'll bet on you to win.
And will you brunch me,
And then lunch me,
Then make me stay to dine?
Yes, 'til from Alpha to Omega, you're mine.

Refrain 5:
From Alpha to Omega,
From A to Z,
From Alpha to Omega,
You're made for me.
From old English Sherry
To very French Vermouth,
From Mozambique to Battle Creek,
Not to mention, from North to South.*
From great eagles to sparrows,
From large to small,
From Austins to big Pierce-Arrows,
Your rumble tops 'em all,
And will you beat me,
And maltreat me,
And bend my Spanish spine?
Yes, 'til from Alpha to Omega you're mine.

*Pronounced Nauth and Sooth.

Act II Finale:
From Martinis to brandy,
From East to West,
From Salomey to Sally Randy,
I like your fan the best,
And from morning until ev'ning,
The sun will never shine,
'Til from Alpha to Omega you're mine.

From This Moment On

Words and Music by Cole Porter

from *Out of This World*

Now that we are close,
No more nights morose,
Now that we are one,
The beguine has just begun.
Now that we're side by side,
The future looks so gay,
Now we are alibied
When we say:

Refrain:
From this moment on,
You for me, dear,
From this moment on,
From this happy day,
No more blue songs,
Only whoop-dee-doo songs,
From this moment on.
For you've got the love I need so much,
Got the skin I love to touch,
Got the arms to hold me tight,
Got the lips to kiss me good night.
From this moment on,
You and I, babe,
We'll be ridin' high, babe,
Every care is gone
From this moment on.

Interlude:
My dear one, my fair one,
My sunbeam, my moonbeam,
My bluebird, my lovebird,
My dreamboat, my cream puff,
My ducky, my wucky,
My poopsy, my woopsy
My tootsy, my wootsy,
My cooky, my wooky,
My piggy, my wiggy,
My sugar, my sweet,
No wonder we rewonder,
We rewonder, we repeat:

Refrain

Get Me to the Church on Time

Words by Alan Jay Lerner
Music by Frederick Loewe

from *My Fair Lady*

I'm getting married in the morning.
Ding! Dong! The bells are gonna chime.
Pull out the stopper;
Let's have a whopper;
But get me to the church on time!
I gotta be there in the morning;
Spruced up and looking in my prime.
Girls, come out and kiss me;
Show how you'll miss me,
But get me to the church on time!

If I am dancing,
Roll up the floor!
If I am whistling,
Whewt me out the door!
For I'm getting married in the morning.
Ding! Dong! The bells are gonna chime.
Kick up a rumpus,
But don't lose the compass,
And get me to the church,
Get me to the church,
For Gawd's sake,
Get me to the church on time.

Gaston

Lyrics by Howard Ashman
Music by Alan Menken

from Walt Disney's *Beauty and the Beast: The Broadway Musical*

LeFou:
Gosh, it disturbs me to see you, Gaston,
Looking so down in the dumps.
Ev'ry guy here'd like to be you, Gaston,
Even when taking your lumps.
There's no man in town as admired as you.
You're ev'ryone's favorite guy.
Ev'ryone's awed and inspired by you,
And it's not very hard to see why.

No one's slick as Gaston.
No one's quick as Gaston.
No one's neck's as incredibly thick as
  Gaston's.
For there's no man in town half as manly.
Perfect! A pure paragon.
You can ask any Tom, Dick or Stanley,
And they'll tell you whose team they prefer to
  play on.
Chorus:
No one's been like Gaston,
A kingpin like Gaston,
LeFou:
No one's got a swell cleft in his chin like
  Gaston.
Gaston:
As a specimen, yes, I'm intimidating!
Chorus:
My, what a guy, that Gaston!
Give five "hurrahs!"
Give twelve "hip-hips!"
LeFou:
Gaston is the best and the rest is all drips!

Men:
No one fights like Gaston,
Douses lights like Gaston,
LeFou:
In a wrestling match, nobody bites like
  Gaston.
Women:
For there's no one as burly and brawny.
Gaston:
As you see, I've got biceps to spare.
LeFou:
Not a bit of him's scraggly or scrawny.
Gaston:
(Spoken) That's right!
And ev'ry last inch of me's covered with hair.
Chorus:
No one hits like Gaston, matches wits like
  Gaston,
LeFou:
In a spitting match, nobody spits like Gaston.
Gaston:
I'm especially good at expectorating. Ptooey!
Chorus:
Ten points for Gaston!

Gaston:
When I was a lad I ate four dozen eggs
Ev'ry morning to help me get large.
And now that I'm grown, I eat five dozen eggs,
So I'm roughly the size of a barge!

Chorus:
No one shoots like Gaston,
Makes those beauts like Gaston.
Then goes tromping around in his boots like Gaston.
Gaston:
I use antlers in all of my decorating!
Chorus:
My, what a guy,
Gaston!

Get Out of Town

Words and Music by Cole Porter

from *Leave It to Me!*

The farce was ended,
The curtains drawn.
And I at least pretended
That love was dead and gone.
But now from nowhere,
You come to me as before,
To take my heart,
And break my heart
Some more.

Get out of town,
Before it's too late, my love,
Get out of town,
Be good to me, please.
Why wish me harm?
Why not retire to a farm,
And be contented to charm
The birds off the trees?

Just disappear,
I care for you much too much.
And when you are near,
Close to me, dear,
We touch too much.
The thrill when we meet
Is so bitter sweet
That darling, it's getting me down.
So on your mark, get set,
Get out of town.

The Girl That I Marry

Words and Music by Irving Berlin

from the Stage Production *Annie Get Your Gun*

The girl that I marry will have to be
As soft and as pink as a nursery.
The girl I call my own,
Will wear satin and laces and smell of cologne.

Her nails will be polished and in her hair,
She'll wear a gardenia. And I'll be there
'Stead of flittin' I'll be sittin'
Next to her and she'll purr like a kitten.

A doll I can carry,
The girl that I marry must be.

Give Him the Oo-La-La

Words and Music by Cole Porter

from *DuBarry Was a Lady*

Refrain:
Say you're fond of fancy things,
Diamond clips and em'rald rings;
If you want your man to come through,
Give him the Oo-la-la!

When your car is asked to stop,
By a handsome traffic cop,
'Less you want a ticket or two,
Give him the Oo-la-la!

If poor Napoleon at the Waterloo-la-la,
Had had an army of debutantes,
To give the British the well known Oo-la-la,
He'd have changed the hist'ry of France.

When your fav'rite Romeo
Grabs his hat and starts to go,
Don't reveal the fact you are blue,
Don't break down and start to boo-hoo.
There's but one thing for you, la-la,
To, la-la,
Do, la-la,
Dance a hula,
And give him the Oo-la-la!
La-la, la-la, la-la,
The Oo-la-la,
The Oo-la-la,
The Oo-la-la, Oo-la-la,
Oo-la-la, Oo-la-la,
Oo-la-la!

Refrain

ADDITIONAL LYRICS
Refrain 2
If the tax man calls one day
And insists you pay and pay,
Just to cut your taxes in two,
Give him the Oo-la-la!

If your rich old uncle Ben,
Starts to make his will again,
Just before his lawyer is due,
Give him the Oo-la-la!

If Mr. Roosevelt desires to rule-la-la,
Until the year nineteen forty-four,
He'd better teach Eleanor how to Oo-la-la!
And he'll be elected once more.

If your bridegroom at the church,
Starts to leave you in the lurch,
Don't proceed to fall in a faint,
Don't run wild and crack up a saint,
There's but one thing for you-la-la,
To, la-la,
Do, la-la,
Go Tallulah,
And give him the Oo-la-la!

Goodnight, My Someone

By Meredith Willson

from Meredith Willson's *The Music Man*

Goodnight my someone, goodnight my love.
Sleep tight, my someone, sleep tight, my love.
Our star is shining its brightest light
For goodnight, my love for goodnight.

Refrain:
Sweet dreams be yours, dear, if dreams there be;
Sweet dreams to carry you close to me.
I wish they may and I wish they might.
Now goodnight, my someone goodnight.

True love can be whispered from heart to heart,
When lovers are parted they say.
But I must depend on a wish and a star,
As long as my heart doesn't know who you are.

Refrain

Hello, Dolly!

Music and Lyric by Jerry Herman

from *Hello, Dolly!*

Dolly:
Hello, Harry,
Well, hello, Louie,
It's so nice to be back home where I belong.
You're lookin' swell, Danny,
I can tell, Manny,
You're still glowin', you're still crowin',
You're still goin' strong.
I feel the room swayin',
For the band's playin'
One of my old fav'rite songs from 'way back when.
So, bridge that gap, fellas,
Find me an empty lap, fellas,
Dolly'll never go away again!

Men:
Hello, Dolly,
Well, hello, Dolly,
It's so nice to have you back where you belong.
You're lookin' swell, Dolly,
We can tell, Dolly,
You're still glowin', you're still crowin',
You're still goin' strong.
We feel the room swayin',
For the band's playin'
One of your old fav'rite songs from 'way back
    when. So,
Dolly:
Here's my hat, fellas,
I'm stayin' where I'm at, fellas.
Men:
Promise you'll never go away again!

Dolly:
I went away from the lights of
    Fourteenth Street,
And into my personal haze.
But now that I'm back in the lights of
    Fourteenth Street,
Tomorrow will be brighter than the
    good old days.
Men:
Those good old days!

Hello, Dolly,
Well, hello (hey, look, there's) Dolly.

Dolly:
(*Spoken*) Glad to see you,
(*Sung*) Hank, let's thank my lucky star.
(Your lucky star.)
(*Spoken*) You're lookin' great, Stanley,
Lose some weight, Stanley?
(*Sung*) Dolly's overjoyed and over-
    whelmed,
And over par.
Men:
I hear the ice tinkle,
See the lights twinkle,
And you still get glances from us hand-
    some men. So,
Dolly:
Golly gee, fellas,
Find me a vacant knee, fellas,
Men:
Dolly'll never go away again.

Men:
Well, well, hello, Dolly,
Well, hello, Dolly,
It's so nice to have you back where you belong.
You're lookin' swell, Dolly,
We can tell, Dolly,
You're still glowin', you're still crowin',
You're still goin' strong.
I hear the ice tinkle,
See the lights twinkle,
And you still get glances from us handsome men. So,
Dolly:
Wa,wa, wow, fellas,
Look at the old girl now, fellas,
Men:
Dolly'll never go away again!

Hello, Young Lovers

Lyrics by Oscar Hammerstein II
Music by Richard Rodgers

from *The King and I*

When I think of Tom
I think about a night
When the earth smelled of summer
And the sky was streaked with white,
And the soft mist of England
Was sleeping on a hill,
I remember this
And I always will.
There are new lovers now
On the same silent hill
Looking on the same blue sea,
And I know Tom and I
Are a part of them all
And they're all a part of Tom and me.

Hello, young lovers,
Whoever you are,
I hope your troubles are few
All my good wishes go with you tonight
I've been in love like you.
Be brave, young lovers, and follow your star,
Be brave and faithful and true.
Cling very close to each other tonight
I've been in love like you.

I know how it feels
To have wings on your heels,
And to fly down a street in a trance
You fly down a street
On a chance that you'll meet,
And you meet
Not really by chance.

Don't cry young lovers,
Whatever you do,
Don't cry because I'm alone.
All of my memories are happy tonight!
I've had a love of my own,
I've had a love of my own like yours,
I've had a love of my own.

Here in My Arms

Words by Lorenz Hart
Music by Richard Rodgers

from *Dearest Enemy*

He:
I know a merry place
Far from intrusion.
It's just the very place
For your seclusion.
There you can while away
Days as you smile away.
It's not a mile away
But it's new to you.

Refrain:
Here in my arms it's adorable.
It's deplorable
That you were never there.
When little lips are kissable
It's permissible
For me to ask my share.
Next to my heart it is ever so lonely,
I'm holding only air,
While here in my arms it's adorable!
It's deplorable
That you were never there.

She:
I know a pretty place
At your command, sir.
It's not a city place,
Yet near at hand, sir.
Here, if you loll away,
Two hearts can toll away.
You'd never stroll away,
If only you knew.

Refrain

Reprise:
Your pretty words were adorable.
It's deplorable
That they were only lies.
Still you will find that I'm affable.
It was laughable
That I believed your eyes.
Next to my heart it is ever so lonely,
I'm holding only air,
While here in my arms it's adorable!
It's deplorable
You will never be there.

Honeysuckle Rose

Words by Andy Razaf
Music by Thomas "Fats" Waller

from *Ain't Misbehavin'*

Every honey bee fills with jealousy
When they see you out with me.
I don't blame them, goodness knows,
Honeysuckle Rose.

When you're passin' by,
Flowers droop and sigh,
And I know the reason why;
You're much sweeter, goodness knows.

Don't buy sugar, you just have to touch my cup.
You're my sugar, it's sweet when you stir it up.
When I'm takin' sips from your tasty lips,
Seems the honey fairly drips.
You're confection, goodness knows,
Honeysuckle Rose.

How Are Things in Glocca Morra

Words by E.Y. Harburg
Music by Burton Lane

from *Finian's Rainbow*

I hear a bird,
Londonderry bird,
It well may be he's bringing me a cheering word.
I hear a breeze,
A River Shannon breeze,
It well may be it's followed me across the seas.
Then tell me please:

How are things in Glocca Morra?
Is that little brook still leaping there?
Does it still run down to Donny cove?
Through Killy begs, Kilkerry and Kildare?
How are things in Glocca Morra?
Is that willow tree still weeping there?
Does that laddie {lassie} with the twinklin' eye
Come whistlin' {smilin'} by
And does he {she} walk away,
Sad and dreamy there not to see me there?
So I ask each weepin' willow
And each brook along the way,
And each lad {lass}
That comes a-whistlin' {a-sighin'} Tooralay:
How are things in Glocca Morra this fine day?

How High the Moon

Words by Nancy Hamilton
Music by Morgan Lewis

from *Two for the Show*

Somewhere there's music,
How faint the tune!
Somewhere there's heaven,
How high the moon!
There is no moon above
When love is far away too,
Till it comes true
That you love me as I love you.

Somewhere's there's music,
It's where you are,
Somewhere there's heaven,
How near, how far!
The darkest night would shine
If you would come to me soon,
Until you will,
How still my heart,
How high the moon!

How to Handle a Woman

Words by Alan Jay Lerner
Music by Frederick Loewe

from *Camelot*

Spoken:
You swore that you had taught me
Ev'rything from A to Zed,
Sung:
With nary an omission in between.
Well, I shall tell you what
You obviously forgot:
That's how a ruler rules a queen!
And what of teaching me
By turning me to animal and bird,
From beaver to the smallest bobolink!
I should have had a whirl
At changing to a girl,
To learn the way the creatures think!

But wasn't there a night,
On a summer long gone by,
We pass'd a couple wrangling away;
And did I not say, Merlyn,
What if that chap were I?
And did he not give counsel and say…
What was it now?
My mind's a wall.
Oh, yes!
By jove, now I recall:

How to handle a woman?
There's a way, said the wise old man;
A way known by ev'ry woman
Since the whole rig'marole began.

Do I flatter her?
I begged him answer.
Do I threaten or cajole or plead?
Do I brood or play the gay romancer?
Said he, smiling:
No indeed.

How to handle a woman?
Mark me well, I will tell you, Sir:
The way to handle a woman
Is to love her, simply love her,
Merely love her…love her…love her.

I Could Have Danced All Night

Words by Alan Jay Lerner
Music by Frederick Loewe

from *My Fair Lady*

I could have danced all night!
I could have danced all night!
And still have begged for more.
I could have spread my wings
And done a thousand things
I've never done before.

I'll never know what made it so exciting.
Why all at once my heart took flight.
I only know when he began to dance with me
I could have danced and danced all night.

I Didn't Know What Time It Was

Words by Lorenz Hart
Music by Richard Rodgers

from *Too Many Girls*

Once I was young
Yesterday, perhaps
Danced with Jim and Paul
And kissed some other chaps.
Once I was young,
But never was naïve.
I thought I had a trick or two
Up my imaginary sleeve.
And now I know I was naïve.

Refrain:
I didn't know what time it was,
Then I met you.
Oh, what a lovely time it was,
How sublime it was, too!
I didn't know what day it was.
You held my hand.
Warm like the month of May it was,
And I'll say it was grand.
Grand to be alive, to be young,
To be mad, to be yours alone!
Grand to see your face, feel your touch,
Hear your voice say I'm all your own.
I didn't know what year it was.
Life was no prize.
I wanted love and here it was
Shining out of your eyes.
I'm wise,
And I know what time it is now.

Once I was old
Twenty years or so
Rather well preserved
The wrinkles didn't show.
Once I was old,
But not too old for fun.
I used to hunt for little girls
With my imaginary grin.
But now I aim for only one!

Refrain

I Do Not Know a Day
I Did Not Love You

Lyrics by Martin Charnin
Music by Richard Rodgers

from *Two by Two*

I do not know a day I did not love you.
I can't remember love not being there.
The planting, when the earth ran through your fingers,
The harvest when the sun danced in your hair.

I do not know a day I did not need you,
For sharing ev'ry moment that I spent.
I needed you before I ever knew you,
Before I knew what needing someone meant.

And if we ever were to have tomorrow,
One fact alone is full (and filled with song),
You will not know a day I do not love you,
The way that I have loved you all along.

I Don't Care Much

Words by Fred Ebb
Music by John Kander

from the Musical *Cabaret*

I don't care much.
Go or stay.
I don't care very much,
Either way.

Hearts grow hard
On a windy street.
Lips grow cold,
With the rent to meet.
So if you kiss me,
If we touch,
Warning's fair,
I don't care very much.

Words sound false
When your coat's too thin,
Feet don't waltz
When the roof caves in.
So if you kiss me,
If we touch,
Warning's fair,
I don't care very much.

I Don't Need Anything but You

Lyric by Martin Charnin
Music by Charles Strouse

from the Musical Production *Annie*

Together at last,
Together forever.
We're tying a knot
They never can sever.
I don't need sunshine now to turn my skies to blue,
I don't need anything but you!

You've wrapped me around
That cute little finger.
You've made life a song,
You've made me the singer,
And what's that bathtub tune you always "bu-bu-boo?"
Ba ba ba, anything but you!

Yesterday was plain awful,
You can say that again.
Yesterday was plain awful,
But that's not now, that's then.

(Annie) I'm poor as a mouse,
(Warbucks) I'm richer than Midas,
But nothing on earth
Could ever divide us,
And if tomorrow I'm an apple seller, too,
I don't need anything but you!

I Dreamed a Dream

Music by Claude-Michel Schönberg
Lyrics by Herbert Kretzmer
Original Text by Alain Boublil and Jean-Marc Natel

from *Les Misérables*

I dreamed a dream in days gone by
When hope was high and life worth living.
I dreamed that love would never die.
I dreamed that God would be forgiving.
Then I was young and unafraid
And dreams were made and used and wasted.
There was no ransom to be paid,
No song unsung, no wine untasted.
But the tigers come at night
With their voices soft as thunder.
As they tear your hope apart,
As they turn your dream to shame.
He slept a summer by my side.
He filled my days with endless wonder.
He took my childhood in his stride.
But he was gone when autumn came.
And still I dreamed he'd come to me,
That we would live the years together.
But there are dreams that cannot be,
And there are storms we cannot weather.
I had a dream my life would be
So different from this hell I'm living,
So different now from what it seemed.
Now life has killed the dream I dreamed.

I Enjoy Being a Girl

Lyrics by Oscar Hammerstein II
Music by Richard Rodgers

from *Flower Drum Song*

I'm a girl and by me that's only great!
I am proud that my silhouette is curvy,
That I walk with a sweet and girlish gait,
With my hips kind of swively and swervy.
I adore being dressed in something frilly
When my date comes to get me at my place.
Out I go with my Joe or John or Billy,
Like a filly who is ready for the race!

When I have a brand new hair-do,
With my eyelashes all in curl,
I float as the clouds on air do,
I enjoy being a girl!

When men say I'm cute and funny,
And my teeth aren't teeth, but pearl,
I just lap it up like honey,
I enjoy being a girl!

I flip when a fellow sends me flowers,
I drool over dresses made of lace,
I talk on the telephone for hours
With a pound and a half of cream upon my
    face!

I'm strictly a female female,
And my future, I hope, will be
In the home of a brave and free male
Who'll enjoy being a guy,
Having a girl like me!

When men say I'm sweet as candy
As around in a dance we whirl,
It goes to my head like brandy,
I enjoy being a girl!

When someone with eyes that smoulder,
Says he loves every silken curl
That falls on my ivory shoulder,
I enjoy being a girl!

When I hear the complimentary whistle
That greets my bikini by the sea,
I turn and I glower and I bristle
But I'm happy to know the whistle's meant
    for me!

I'm strictly a female female,
And my future, I hope, will be
In the home of a brave and free male
Who'll enjoy being a guy,
Having a girl like me.

I Had Myself a True Love

Words by Johnny Mercer
Music by Harold Arlen

from *St. Louis Woman*

I had myself a true love,
A true love who was somethin' to see
I had myself a true love,
At least that's what I kept on tellin' me,

First thing in the mornin'
I still try to think up a way to be with him,
Some part of the evenin'
An' that's the way I live thru the day.
She had herself a true love,
But now he's gone an' left her for good.

Lord knows, I done heard those backyard whispers
Goin' 'round the neighborhood.
There may be a lot of things I miss,
A lot of things I don't know, but I do know this:
Now I ain't got no love
An' once upon a time I had a true love

In the evening!
In the doorway,
While I stand there and wait for his comin'.
With the house swept,
And the clothes hung,
An' the pot on the stove there a-hummin',
Where is he, while I watch the risin' moon?
With that gal in that damn ol' saloon?

No! That ain't the way that it used to be.
No! An' everybody keeps tellin' me,
There may be a lot o' things I miss.
A lot o' things I don't know, but I do know this:
Now I ain't got no love
An' once upon a time I had a true love.

I Hate Men

Words and Music by Cole Porter

from *Kiss Me, Kate*

I hate men,
I can't abide 'em even now and then.
Than ever marry one of them,
I'd rest a virgin rather,
For husbands are a boring lot,
And only give you bother.
Of course, I'm awf'lly glad
That mother had to marry father.

But I hate men.
Of all the types I've ever met,
Within our democracy,
I hate the most the athlete
With his manner bold and brassy.
He may have hair upon his chest,
But sister, so has Lassie,
Oh, I hate men!

I hate men,
Their worth upon this earth I dinna ken.
Avoid the trav'lling salesman,
Though a tempting Tom he may be,
From China he will bring you jade,
And perfume from Araby.
But don't forget 'tis he who'll have the fun,
And thee the baby.

Oh, I hate men.
If thou shouldst wed a bus'ness man,
Be wary, oh be wary,
He'll tell you he's detained in town
On bus'ness necessary.
His bus'ness is the bus'ness
Which he gives his secretary,
Oh, I hate men!

I Love a Piano

Words and Music by Irving Berlin

from the Stage Production *Stop! Look! Listen!*

As a child,
I went wild
When a band played.
How I ran
To the man
When his hand swayed.
Clarinets
Were my pets,
And a slide trombone
I thought was simply divine.
But today
When they play
I could hiss them.
Every bar
Is a jar
To my system.
But there's one musical instrument
That I call mine.

When a green
Tetrazine
Starts to warble,
I grow cold
As an old
Piece of marble.
I allude
To the crude
Little party singer,
Who don't know when to pause.

At her best
I detest
The soprano,
But I run
To the one
At the piano.
I always love the accomp'niment
And that's because,

I love a piano
I love a piano.
I love to hear somebody play
Upon a piano
A grand piano.
It simply carries me away.

I know a fine way
To treat a Steinway.
I love to run my fingers o'er the keys
The ivories.
And with the pedal
I love to meddle
Not only music from Broadway.*
I'm so delighted
If I'm invited
To hear a long-haired genius play.
So you can keep your fiddle
And your bow.
Give me a p-i-a-n-o. Oh, Oh
I love to stop right
Beside an upright
Or high toned baby grand.

Original: When Paderewski comes this way.

I Remember It Well

Words by Alan Jay Lerner
Music by Frederick Loewe

from *Gigi*

He: We met at nine.
She: We met at eight.
He: I was on time.
She: No, you were late.
He: Ah yes! I remember it well.
He: We dined with friends.
She: We dined alone.
He: A tenor sang.
She: A baritone.
He: Ah yes! I remember it well.

He: That sizzling April moon!
She: There was none that night,
And the month was June.
He: That's right! That's right!
She: It warms my heart to know that you
Remember still the way you do.
He: Ah yes! I remember it well.

He: How often I've thought of that Friday
She: Monday night,
He: When we had our last rendezvous.
And somehow I've foolishly wondered if you might
By some chance be thinking of it too?

He: That carriage ride.
She: You walked me home.
He: You lost a glove.
She: I lost a comb.

He: Ah yes! I remember it well..
The brilliant sky.
She: We had some rain.
He: Those Russian songs
She: From sunny Spain?
He: Ah yes! I remember it well.

He: You wore a gown of gold.
She: I was all in blue.
He: Am I getting old?
She: Oh no! Not you!
How strong you were, how young
    and gay;
A prince of love in every way.
He: Ah yes! I remember it well.

I Whistle a Happy Tune

Lyrics by Oscar Hammerstein II
Music by Richard Rodgers

from *The King and I*

Whenever I feel afraid
I hold my head erect
And whistle a happy tune,
So no one will suspect
I'm afraid.

While shivering in my shoes
I strike a careless pose
And whistle a happy tune,
And no one ever knows
I'm afraid.

The result of this deception
Is very strange to tell,
For when I fool the people I fear
I fool myself as well!

I whistle a happy tune,
And every single time
The happiness in the tune
Convinces me that I'm
Not afraid!

Make believe you're brave
And the trick will take you far;
You may be as brave
As you make believe you are.
You may be as brave
As you make believe you are.

I Wish I Were in Love Again

Words by Lorenz Hart
Music by Richard Rodgers

from *Babes in Arms*

You don't know that I felt good
When we up and parted.
You don't know I knocked on wood,
Gladly broken-hearted.
Worrying is through,
I sleep all night,
Appetite and health restored.
You don't know how much I'm bored.

Refrain 1:
The sleepless nights,
The daily fights,
The quick toboggan when you reach the
   heights
I miss the kisses and I miss the bites.
I wish I were in love again!
The broken dates,
The endless waits,
The lovely loving and the hateful hates,
The conversation with the flying plates
I wish I were in love again!
No more pain,
No more strain,
Now I'm sane but…
I would rather be gaga!
The pulled-out fur
Of cat and cur,
The fine mis-mating of a him and her
I've learned my lesson, but I wish I were
In love again!

Refrain 2:
The furtive sigh,
The blackened eye,
The words "I'll love you till the day I die,"
The self-deception that believes the lie
I wish I were in love again.
When love congeals
It soon reveals
The faint aroma of performing seals,
The double-crossing of a pair of heels.
I wish I were in love again!
No more care.
No despair.
I'm all there now,
But I'd rather be punch-drunk!
Believe me, sir,
I much prefer
The classic battle of a him and her.
I don't like quiet and I wish I were
In love again.

I Won't Send Roses

Music and Lyric by Jerry Herman

from *Mack and Mabel*

I won't send roses,
Or hold the door,
I won't remember
Which dress you wore.
My heart is too much in control.
The lack of romance in my soul
Will turn you gray, kid,
So stay away, kid.

Forget my shoulder
When you're in need.
Forgetting birthdays
Is guaranteed.
And should I love you,
You would be the last to know.
I won't send roses,
And roses suit you so.

My pace is frantic,
My temper's cross.
With words romantic,
I'm at a loss.
I'd be the first one to agree
That I'm preoccupied with me.
And it's inbred, kid,
So keep your head, kid.

In me you'll find things
Like guts and nerve,
But not the kind things
That you deserve.
And so while there's a fighting chance,
Just turn and go.
I won't send roses,
And roses suit you so.

I'm Gonna Sit Right Down and Write Myself a Letter

Lyric by Joe Young
Music by Fred E. Ahlert

from *Ain't Misbehavin'*

I'm gonna sit right down and write myself a letter
And make believe it came from you.
I'm gonna write words, oh so sweet,
They're gonna knock me off my feet.
A lot of kisses on the bottom,
I'll be glad I got 'em.
I'm gonna smile and say, "I hope you're feeling better"
And close "with love" the way you do.
I'm gonna sit right down and write myself a letter
And make believe it came from you.

I've Come to Wive It Wealthily in Padua

Words and Music by Cole Porter

from *Kiss Me, Kate*

Petruchio:
I've come to wive it wealthily in Padua,
If wealthily then happily in Padua,
If my wife has a bag of gold,
Do I care if the bag is old?
I've come to wive it wealthily in Padua.
Chorus:
He's come to wive it wealthily in Padua.

Petruchio:
I heard you mutter, "Zounds, a loathsome
   lad you are."
I shall not be disturbed a bit,
If she be but a quarter wit.
If she can only talk of clo'es
While she powders her doggone nose.
I've come to wive it wealthily in Padua.
Chorus:
He's come to wive it wealthily in Padua.

Petruchio:
I heard you say, "Gadzooks, completely mad
   you are."
'Twouldn't give me the slightest shock,
If her knees, now and then, should knock,
If her eyes were a wee bit crossed,
Were she wearing the hair she'd lost,
Still the damsel I'll make my dame,
In the dark they are all the same.
I've come to wive it wealthily in Padua.
Chorus:
He's come to wive it wealthily in Padua.

Petruchio:
I heard you say, "Good gad, but what a cad
   you are."
Do I mind if she fret and fuss,
If she fume like Vesuvius,
If she roar like a winter breeze
On the rough Adriatic seas,
If she scream like a teething brat,
If she scratch like a tiger cat,
If she fight like a raging boar?
I have oft stuck a pig before.
I've come to wive it wealthily in Padua.

Chorus:
With a Hunny, nunny, nunny,
And a hey, hey, hey.
Petruchio:
Not to mention money, money,
For a rainy day.
Petruchio and Chorus:
I've [He's] come to wive it wealthily in
   Padua.

I've Grown Accustomed to Her Face

Words by Alan Jay Lerner
Music by Frederick Loewe

from *My Fair Lady*

I've grown accustomed to her face
She almost makes the day begin.
I've grown accustomed to the tune,
She whistles night and noon,
Her smiles, her frowns,
Her ups, her downs
Are second nature to me now;
Like breathing out and breathing in.
I was serenely independent
And content before we met;
Surely, I could always
Be that way again and yet,
I've grown accustomed to her looks;
Accustomed to her voice
Accustomed to her face.

I've grown accustomed to her face
She almost makes the day begin.
I've gotten used to hear her say:
"Good morning" every day,
Her joys, her woes,
Her highs, her lows
Are second nature to me now;
Like breathing out and breathing in.
I'm very grateful she's a woman
And so easy to forget
Rather like a habit
One can always break and yet,
I've grown accustomed to the trace
Of something in the air;
Accustomed to her face.

I've Never Been in Love Before

By Frank Loesser

from *Guys and Dolls*

I've never been in love before,
Now all at once it's you.
It's you forever more.

I've never been in love before.
I thought my heart was safe,
I thought I knew the score.

But this is wine that's all too strange and strong.
I'm full of foolish song, and out my song must pour.
So please forgive this helpless haze I'm in.
I've really never been in love before.

If I Can't Love Her

Music by Alan Menken
Lyrics by Tim Rice

from *Walt Disney's Beauty and the Beast: The Broadway Musical*

And in my twisted face,
There's not the slightest trace
Of anything that even hints of kindness.
And from my tortured shape,
No comfort, no escape.
I see, but deep within is utter blindness.
Hopeless, as my dream dies.
As the time flies, love a lost illusion.
Helpless, unforgiven.
Cold and driven to this sad conclusion.

No beauty could move me,
No goodness improve me.
No power on Earth,
If I can't love her.
No passion could reach me,
No lesson could teach me
How I could have loved her,
And make her love me too.
If I can't love her, then who?

Long ago, I should have seen
All the things I could have been.
Careless and unthinking,
I moved onward!

No pain could be deeper.
No life could be cheaper.
No point anymore,
If I can't love her.
No spirit could win me.
No hope left within me,
Hope I could have loved her,
And that she'd set me free.
But it's not to be.
If I can't love her,
Let the world be done with me.

If I Ruled the World

Words by Leslie Bricusse
Music by Cyril Ornadel

from *Pickwick*

If I ruled the world
Every day would be the first day of spring,
Every heart would have a new song to sing
And we'd sing of the joy every morning would bring.

If I ruled the world
Every man would be as free as a bird,
Every voice would be a voice to be heard.
Take my word we would treasure each day that occurred.

My world would be a beautiful place
Where we would weave such wonderful dreams.
My world would wear a smile on its face
Like the man in the moon has when the moon beams.

If I ruled the world
Every man would say the world was his friend.
There'd be happiness that no man could end.
No, my friend, not if I ruled the world.
Every head would be held up high.
There'd be sunshine in everyone's sky
If the day ever dawned when I ruled the world.

If I Were a Bell

By Frank Loesser

from *Guys and Dolls*

Ask me how do I feel,
Ask me now that we're cozy and clinging.
Well sir, all I can say is
If I were a bell I'd be ringing.
From the moment we kissed tonight
That's the way I've just got to behave.
Boy, if I were a lamp I'd light
Or if I were a banner I'd wave.

Ask me how do I feel,
Little me with my quiet upbringing.
Well sir, all I can say is
If I were a gate I'd be swinging.
And if I were a watch I'd start popping my spring.
Or if I were a bell I'd go ding dong ding dong ding.

Ask me how do I feel
From this chemistry lesson I'm learning.
Well sir, all I can say is
If I were a bridge I'd be burning.
Yes, I knew my morale would crack
From the wonderful way you looked.
Boy, if I were a duck I'd quack
Or if I were a goose I'd be cooked.

Ask me how do I feel,
Ask me now that we're fondly caressing.
Pal, if I were a salad
I know I would be splashing my dressing.
Or if I were a season I'd surely be spring.
Or if I were a bell I'd go ding dong ding dong ding.

If This Isn't Love

Words by E.Y. Harburg
Music by Burton Lane

from *Finian's Rainbow*

A secret, a secret,
She says she's got a secret.
A secret, a secret,
A secret kind of secret.
She's aching for to shout it
To ev'ry daffodil,
And tell the world about it,
In fact she says she will.
She says?
She says:

If this isn't love,
The whole world is crazy.
If this isn't love,
I'm daft as a daisy.
With moons all around,
And cows jumping over,
There's something amiss,
And I'll eat my hat
If this isn't love.

I'm feelin' like the apple
On top of William Tell;
With this I cannot grapple,
Because,
Because,
You're so adorable.

If this isn't love,
Then winter is summer.
(Yes, winter's summer.)
If this isn't love,
My heart needs a plumber.
(His heart needs a plumber.)

I'm swingin' on stars,
I'm ridin' on rainbows,
(He rides, he rides a rainbow.)
I'm bustin' with bliss,
And I'll kiss your hand
If this isn't love.

If this isn't love,
There's no Gloccamorra.
If this isn't love,
I'm Zha Zha Gabora.
If this is a dream,
And if I should wake up,
Will you hear a hiss,
Will my face be red,
If this isn't love.

I'm gettin' tired of waitin'
And stickin' to the rules.
This feelin' calls for matin',
Like birds and bees and other animules.

If this isn't love,
We're all seeing double.
If this isn't love,
I'm really in trouble.
If she's not the girl,
And he's not the hero.
A kiss ain't a kiss,
It's a crisis, man,
If this isn't love.

If You Could See Her

Words by Fred Ebb
Music by John Kander

from the Musical *Cabaret*

I know what you're thinking.
You wonder why I chose her.
Out of all the ladies in the world.
That's just a first impression,
What good's a first impression?
If you knew her like I do,
It would change your point of view.

If you could see her through my eyes,
You wouldn't wonder at all.
If you could see her through my eyes,
I guarantee you would fall (like I did).
When we're in public together,
I hear society moan.
But if they could see her through my eyes,
Maybe they'd leave us alone.

How can I speak of her virtues?
I don't know where to begin.
She's clever, she's smart, she reads music,
She doesn't smoke or drink gin (like I do).
Yet, when we're walking together,
They sneer if I'm holding her hand.
But if they could see her through my eyes,
Maybe they'd all understand.

I understand your objection.
I grant you the problem's not small.
But if you could see her through my eyes,
She wouldn't look Jewish at all.

If You Really Knew Me

Words by Carole Bayer Sager
Music by Marvin Hamlisch

from *They're Playing Our Song*

If you* really knew me,
If you really, truly knew me,
Maybe you would see
The other side of me I seldom see.

If there were no music,
If your melody stopped playing,
Would he be the kind of man (girl)
I'd want to see tonight?

Does the man (girl) make the music
Or does the music make the man (girl)?
And am I ev'rything I thought I'd be?

If you really knew me,
If you'd take the time to understand,
Maybe you could find me,
The part I left behind me,
Maybe you'd remind me of who I am.

* Female singers may substitute "he" wherever "you" appears.
  Male singers may substitute "she" wherever "you" appears.

In My Own Little Corner

Lyrics by Oscar Hammerstein II
Music by Richard Rodgers

from *Cinderella*

I'm as mild and meek as a mouse,
When I hear a command I obey.
But I know of a spot in my house
Where no one can stand in my way.

In my own little corner, in my own little
   chair,
I can be whatever I want to be.
On the wing of my fancy I can fly anywhere
And the world will open its arms to me.

I'm a young Norwegian princess or a milk-
   maid,
I'm the greatest prima donna in Milan,
I'm an heiress who has always had her silk
   made
By her own flock of silkworms in Japan!

I'm a girl men go mad for,
Love's a game I can play
With a cool and confident kind of air,
Just as long as I stay in my own little corner,
All alone in my own little chair.

I can be whatever I want to be.
I'm a slave in Calcutta,
I'm a queen in Peru,
I'm a mermaid dancing upon the sea.

I'm a huntress on an African safari
(It's a dang'rous type of sport and yet it's
   fun;)
In the night I sally forth to seek my quarry,
And I find I forgot to bring my gun!

I am lost in the jungle
All alone and unarmed
When I meet a lioness in her lair!
Then I'm glad to be back in my own little
   corner,
All alone in my own little chair.

It Ain't Etiquette

Words and Music by Cole Porter

from *DuBarry Was a Lady*

He:
Missus Emily Post who they tell me
Is most reliable,
She:
Yes, my man of all men.
He:
For a helluva sum
Wrote a book that's become my Bi-a-ble.
She:
So you read now and then.
He:
And if only you look at that
Etiquette book of dear Emily's,
She:
Yes, but how many books?
He:
You can cohabitate with
America's great families,
Now for instance, snooks!

Refrain:
If you meet J.P. Morgan while playing golf
With the Long Island banking set,
Don't greet him by tearing your girdle off,
It ain't etiquette!
When invited to hear from an o'pra box
Rigoletto's divine quartet,
Don't bother your neighbors by throwing
    rocks,
It ain't etiquette.

When you're asked up to dine by
    some mean old minx,
And a meatball is all you get,
Never say to your hostess,
"This dinner stinks,"
It ain't smart,
It ain't chic,
It ain't etiquette.

ADDITIONAL LYRICS
If a very proud mother asks what you think
Of her babe in the bassinette,
Don't tell her it looks like the missing link,
It ain't etiquette.
If you're asked up to tea at Miss Flinch's
    school
By some shy little violet,
Don't pinch poor Miss Flinch in the
    vestibule,
It ain't etiquette.
If you're swimming at Newport with some
    old leech
And he wrestles you while you're wet,
Don't call him a son of a Bailey's Beach,
It ain't smart,
It ain't chic,
It ain't etiquette.

It Was Written in the Stars

Words and Music by Cole Porter

from *DuBarry Was a Lady*

It was written in the stars
That our love would be born;
It was written in the stars
We'd meet early one morn'.
So when first I saw you appear
As the night left the sea,
This was no coincidence, dear.
It was fated to be.

In the heavens high above,
Where dreams flourish and flow'r,
It was written that our love
Would grow stronger each hour.
So remember, when at last, you are mine,
And Venus is mated to Mars,
It was written,
Always written in the stars!

It's a Grand Night for Singing

Lyrics by Oscar Hammerstein II
Music by Richard Rodgers

from *State Fair*

It's a grand night for singing,
The moon is flying high,
And somewhere a bird who is bound he'll be heard,
Is throwing his heart at the sky.
It's a grand night for singing,
The stars are bright above,
The earth is aglow, and, to add to the show,
I think I am falling in love,
Falling, falling in love.

It's a Lovely Day for a Murder

Words by Lorenz Hart
Music by Richard Rodgers

from *Higher and Higher*

Have you ever heard of Saint Bartholomew's Day?
Or the day when they took our liquor away?
Or the day when we have our taxes to pay?
Or the day when the Trojans were fooled by Ulysses?
Well, today is a day,
That makes those days look like sissies.

What a lovely day for a murder,
I could spit!
If there's any day for a murder,
This is it!

Oh, we'll never visit the parson,
So I say,
For seduction, robb'ry and arson,
What a day!

I could choke my grandmother
With her shawl,
I could turn Republican
In the fall.

Oh, it gets absurd and absurder,
So I say,
If you care to join me in murder, Buster,
It's the loveliest day!

It's a Lovely Day Today

Words and Music by Irving Berlin

from the Stage Production *Call Me Madam*

Kenneth:
It's a lovely day today,
So whatever you've got to do,
You've got a lovely day to do it in, that's true.
And I hope whatever you've got to do
Is something that can be done by two,
For I'd really like to stay.
It's a lovely day today,
And whatever you've got to do,
I'd be so happy to be doing it with you.
But if you've got something that must be
  done,
And it can only be done by one,
There is nothing more to say,
Except it's a lovely day for saying
It's a lovely day.

Princess Maria:
It's a lovely day today,
And whatever I've got to do,
I've got a lovely day to do it in, that's true.
But perhaps whatever I've got to do
Is something that can be done by two,
If it is then you could stay.
It's a lovely day today,
But you're probably busy, too,
So I suppose there's nothing we can do.
For if you've got something that must be
  done,
And it can only be done by one,
There is nothing more to say,
Except it's a lovely day for saying
It's a lovely day.

Kenneth:
It's a lovely day today.
If you've something that must be done,
Now don't forget two heads are better than
  one,
And besides I'm certain if you knew me,
You'd find I'm very good company.
Won't you kindly let me stay?

Princess Maria (Spoken):
Mr. American,
Your Madam Ambassador
Asked me to come and see her.
If it were known I did,
There would be a great scandal.

Kenneth: But if you use that passage from
  the Palace—
Princess Maria: Yes, that just occurred to
  me.
Kenneth: And I could be there waiting for
  you.
Princess Maria: That also occurred to me.
Kenneth (Sung): So there's nothing more to
  say,

Both (Sung):
Except it's a lovely day for saying
It's a lovely day.

Kenneth (Spoken):
See you later!

It's All Right with Me

Words and Music by Cole Porter

from *Can-Can*

It's the wrong time and the wrong place,
Though your face is charming, it's the wrong face,
It's not her face, but such a charming face,
That it's all right with me.

It's the wrong song in the wrong style,
Though your smile is lovely, it's the wrong smile,
It's not her smile, but such a lovely smile,
That it's all right with me.

You can't know how happy I am that we met,
I'm strangely attracted to you,
There's someone I'm trying so hard to forget,
Don't you want to forget someone too?

It's the wrong game with the wrong chips,
Though your lips are tempting, they're the wrong lips,
They're not her lips, but they're such tempting lips,
That if some night you're free,
Dear, it's all right,
It's all right with me.

It's Only a Paper Moon

Lyric by Billy Rose and E.Y. Harburg
Music by Harold Arlen

from the Musical Production *The Great Magoo*
originally titled "If You Believed in Me," the newly titled song was featured in the film *Take a Chance*;
  also featured in the film *Paper Moon*

I never feel a thing is real,
When I'm away from you.
Out of your embrace,
The world's a temporary parking place.
A bubble for a minute,
You smile, the bubble has a rainbow in it.

Say, it's only a paper moon,
Sailing over a cardboard sea,
But it wouldn't be make believe,
If you believed in me.

Yes, it's only a canvas sky,
Hanging over a muslin tree,
But it wouldn't be make believe,
If you believed in me.

Without your love,
It's a honky-tonk parade,
Without your love,
It's a melody played in a penny arcade.

It's a Barnum and Bailey world,
Just as phony as it can be,
But it wouldn't be make believe
If you believed in me.

It's the Hard-Knock Life

Lyric by Martin Charnin
Music by Charles Strouse

from the Musical Production *Annie*

It's a hard-knock life for us!
It's a hard-knock life for us!
'Stead-a treated we got tricked.
'Stead-a kisses we got kicked.
It's the hard-knock life!

Got no folds to speak of, so,
It's the hard-knock row we hoe,
Cotton blankets 'stead-a wool,
Empty bellies 'stead-a full,
It's the hard-knock life.

Don't it feel like this wind is always howlin'?
Don't it seem like there's never any light?
Once a day don't you want to throw the
    towel in?
It's easier than puttin' up a fight.
No one's there when your dreams at night
    get creepy,
No one cares if you grow or if you shrink,
No one cries when your eyes get red and
    weepy.
From the cryin' you would think this place
    would sink.
Oh!

Empty belly life!
Rotten smelly life!
Full of sorrow life!
No tomorrow life!

Santa Claus we never see,
Santa Claus, what's that? Who's he?
No one cares for you a smidge,
When you're in an orphanage!
It's a hard knock life.

Yank the whiskers from her chin.
Jab her with a safety pin.
Make her drink a Mickey Finn.
I love you, Miss Hannigan.

It's the hard-knock life for us.
It's the hard-knock life for us.
No one cares for you a smidge,
When you're in an orphanage!
It's the hard knock life.

The Joint Is Jumpin'

Words by Andy Razaf and J.C. Johnson
Music by Thomas "Fats" Waller

from *Ain't Misbehavin'*

They have a new expression along old
   Harlem way,
That tells you when a party is ten times more
   than gay.
To say that things are jumpin' leaves not a
   single doubt,
That everything is in full swing when you
   hear a body shout:
Spoken: (Here 'tis)

The joint is jumpin',
It's really jumpin'.
Come in cats an' check your hats,
I mean this joint is jumpin'.

The piano's thumpin',
The dancers bumpin'.
This here spot is more than hot,
In fact the joint is jumpin'.

Check your weapons at the door,
Be sure to pay your quarter.
Burn your leather on the floor,
Grab anybody's daughter.

The roof is rockin',
The neighbor's knockin'.
We're all bums when the wagon comes.
I mean this joint is jumpin'.
Spoken: (Let it beat!)

The joint is jumpin',
It's really jumpin'.
Every Mose is on his toes,
I mean the joint is jumpin'.

No time for talkin',
It's time for walkin'. (Yes!)
Grab a jug and cut the rug,
I mean this joint is jumpin'.

Get your pig feet, beer and gin,
There's plenty in the kitchen.
Who is that that just came in?
Just look at the way he's switchin'.

Don't mind the hour,
'Cause I'm in power.
I got bail if we go to jail.
I mean the joint is jumpin'.

The joint is jumpin',
It's really jumpin'.
We're all bums when the wagon comes,
I mean this joint is jumpin'.

Spoken:
(Don't give your right name. No, No, No!)

Just a Housewife

Music and Lyric by Craig Carnelia

from the Broadway Musical *Working*

All I am is just a housewife.
Nothing special, nothing great.
What I do is kinda boring.
If you'd rather, it can wait.

All I am is someone's mother.
All I am is someone's wife.
All of which seems unimportant.
All it is is just my life.

Do the laundry, wash the dishes.
Take the dog out, clean the house.
Shop for groc'ries, look for specials.
God, it sounds so Mickey Mouse.

Drop the kids off, pick the shirts up.
Try to lose weight, try again.
Keep the troops fed, pick their things up.
Lose your patience, count to ten.
(Spoken) Two, three, four, five, six,
Seven, eight, nine, ten.
Four, five, six, seven, eight, nine...

All I am is just a housewife.
Just a housewife, nothing great.
What I do is out of fashion.
What I feel is out of date.

All I am is someone's mother.
Right away I'm "not too bright."
What I do is "unfulfilling."
So the T.V. talk shows tell me ev'ry night.

I don't mean to complain and all,
But they make you feel
Like you're two feet tall,
When you're just a wife.
Nowadays all the magazines
Make a bunch o' beans
Out o' fam'ly life.
You're a wiz if you go to work,
But you're just a jerk
If you say you won't.
Women's Lib says they think it's fine
If the choice is mine,
But you know they don't!

What I do, what I *choose* to do,
May be dumb to you,
But it's not to me.
Is it dumb that they need me there?
Is it dumb to care?
'Cause I do, you see.
And I mean, did ya ever think,
Really stop and think
What a job it was,
Doing all the things
That a housewife does?

I'm afraid it's unimpressive.
All I am is someone's mother,
Nothing special,
What I do is unexciting,
Kinda dull.
Take the kids here,
Take the kids there.
I don't mean to complain and all.

All I am is busy, busy.
All I am is like my mother.
All I am is just a housewife.

Kate the Great

Words and Music by Cole Porter

from *Anything Goes*

Katherine of Russia, that potentate,
Knew that her job was to fascinate.
Some people called her a reprobate,
But still she's known as Kate the Great.
To sessions of congress she wouldn't go,
Never heckled the crowd on the radio.
She never would mix in affairs of state,
But in affairs of the heart, how Kate was
    great!

As few lovely ladies today,
She knew where a woman should stay.
She never laid a five-year plan,
But was there ever such a girl,
At laying a plan
For a man?
So drink to that jovial jade
And think of the hist'ry she made.

Why, she made the congress,
She made the premier,
She made the clergy,
And she made 'em cheer.
She made the butler,
She made the groom,
She made the maid,
Who made the room.
She made the army,
She made the marines,
Made some of them princes,
And some of them queens.
And when she was still discontent,
Kate'd create a new regiment.

So, beautiful ladies, before too late,
Follow the lead of this potentate,
Give up arranging affairs of state,
And stay in the hay like Kate the Great,
Hay-de-hay!
Hay-de-hay!
Hay-de-hay!
Hay-de-hay!
So stay in the hay like Kate the Great!

Lazy Afternoon

Words and Music by John Latouche and Jerome Moross

from *The Golden Apple*

It's a lazy afternoon
And the beetle bugs are zoomin'
And the tulip trees are bloomin'
And there's not another human
In view
But us two.
It's a lazy afternoon
And the farmer leaves his reapin',
In the meadow cows are sleepin'
And the speckled trout stop leapin' upstream
As we dream.

A fat pink cloud hangs over the hill,
Unfoldin' like a rose.
If you hold my hand and sit real still
You can hear the grass as it grows.
It's a hazy afternoon
And I know a place that's quiet
'Cept for daisies running riot
And there's no one passing by it to see.
Come spend this lazy afternoon with me.

Leaning on a Lamp Post

By Noel Gay

from *Me and My Girl*

Leaning on a lamp,
Maybe you think I look a tramp,
Or you may think I'm hanging 'round to steal a car.
But no, I'm not a crook,
And if you think that's what I look,
I'll tell you why I'm here and what my motives are.

I'm leaning on a lamp-post
At the corner of the street,
In case a certain lady comes by.
Oh me,
Oh my.
I hope the little lady comes by.

I don't know if she'll get away,
She doesn't always get away,
But anyway I know that she'll try.
Oh me,
Oh my,
I hope the little lady comes by.

Refrain:
There's no other girl I could wait for,
But this one I'd break any date for,
I won't have to ask what she's late for,
She wouldn't leave me flat,
She's not a girl like that.
She's absolutely wonderful and marvelous and beautiful,
And anyone can understand why
I'm leaning on a lamp-post at the corner of the street,
In case a certain little lady comes by.

Refrain

Let Me Entertain You

Words by Stephen Sondheim
Music by Jule Styne

from *Gypsy*

Let me entertain you.
Let me make you smile.
Let me do a few tricks,
Some old and then some new tricks,
I'm very versatile.

And if you're real good,
I'll make you feel good.
I want your spirits to climb.
So let me entertain you,
And we'll have a real good time,
Yes, sir!
We'll have a real good time.

Let me entertain you,
And we'll have a real good time,
Yes, sir!
We'll have a real good time.

Let me do a few tricks,
Some old and then some new tricks.

And if you're real good,
I'll make you feel good.
I want your spirits to climb.
Let me entertain you,
And we'll have a real good time,
Yes, sir!
We'll have a real good time.

A Little Fall of Rain

Music by Claude-Michel Schönberg
Lyrics by Herbert Kretzmer
Original Text by Alain Boublil and Jean-Marc Natel

from *Les Misérables*

Eponine:
Don't you fret, M'sieur Marius,
I don't feel any pain.
A little fall of rain
Can hardly hurt me now.
You're here, that's all I need to know.
And you will keep me safe,
And you will keep me close.
And rain will make the flowers grow.

Marius:
But you will live, 'Ponine,
Dear God above.
If I could close your wounds
With words of love.
Eponine:
Just hold me now and let it be.
Shelter me, comfort me.
Marius:
You would live a hundred years,
If I could show you how.
I won't desert you now.

Eponine:
The rain can't hurt me now.
This rain will wash away what's past.
And you will keep me safe.
And you will keep me close.
I'll sleep in your embrace at last.

The rain that brings you here
Is heaven blessed.
The skies begin to clear,
And I'm at rest.
A breath away from where you are,
I've come home from so far.

So don't you fret, M'sieur Marius,
I don't feel any pain.
A little fall of rain
Can hardly hurt me now.
Marius:
I'm here.
Eponine:
That's all I need to know.
And you will keep me safe.
And you will keep me close.
And rain will make the flowers...
Marius:
Grow.

Little Girl Blue

Words by Lorenz Hart
Music by Richard Rodgers

from *Jumbo*

Verse 1:
Sit there and count your fingers,
What can you do?
Old girl you're through.
Sit there and count your little fingers,
Unlucky little girl blue.

Verse 2:
Sit there and count the raindrops
Falling on you.
It's time you knew,
All you can count on is the raindrops
That fall on little girl blue.

No use, old girl,
You may as well surrender.
Your hope is getting slender,
Why won't somebody send a tender
Blue boy to cheer a little girl blue?

When I was very young
The world was younger than I.
As merry as a carousel
The circus tent was strung
With every star in the sky
Above the ring I love as well.

Now the young world has grown old,
Gone are the tinsel and gold.

Repeat Verses 1 and 2

Long Before I Knew You

Words by Betty Comden and Adolph Green
Music by Jule Styne

from *Bells Are Ringing*

Dearest, dearest,
One thing I know,
Ev'rything I feel for you
Started many years ago.

Long before I knew you,
Long before I met you,
I was sure I'd find you
Some day, somehow.
I pictured someone who'd walk and talk
And smile as you do,
Who'd make me feel as you do,
Right now.

All that was long before I held you,
Long before I kissed you,
Long before I touched you,
And felt this glow.
But now you really are here,
And now at last I know
That long before I knew you,
I loved you so.

Losing My Mind

Words and Music by Stephen Sondheim

from *Follies*

The sun comes up,
I think about you.
The coffee cup,
I think about you.
I want you so,
It's like I'm losing my mind.

The morning ends,
I think about you.
I talk to friends,
I think about you.
And do they know?
It's like I'm losing my mind.

Refrain:
All afternoon,
Doing every little chore.
The thought of you stays bright.
Sometimes I stand in the middle of the floor,
Not going left,
Not going right.
I dim the lights
And think about you,
Spend sleepless nights
To think about you.
You said you loved me,
Or were you just being kind?
Or am I losing my mind?

I want you so,
It's like I'm losing my mind.
Does no one know?
It's like I'm losing my mind.

Refrain

Love Me or Leave Me

Lyrics by Gus Kahn
Music by Walter Donaldson

from *Whoopee!*

Love me or leave me, and let me be lonely;
You won't believe me, and I love you only;
I'd rather be lonely,
Than happy with somebody else.

You might find the night-time, the right time for kissing;
But night-time is my time for just reminiscing,
Regretting, instead of forgetting
With somebody else.

There'll be no one unless that someone is you,
I intend to be independently blue.
I want your love, but I don't want to borrow,
To have it today, and to give back tomorrow;
For my love is your love,
There's no love for nobody else!

Luck Be a Lady

By Frank Loesser

from *Guys and Dolls*

They call you Lady Luck, but there is room for doubt;
At times you have a very unladylike way of running out.
You're on a date with me, the pickings have been lush,
And yet before this evening is over,
You might give me the brush.
You might forget your manners, you might refuse to stay,
And so the best that I can do is pray.

Luck be a lady tonight.
Luck be a lady tonight.
Luck, if you've ever been a lady to begin with,
Luck be a lady tonight.

Luck, let a gentleman see,
How nice a dame you can be.
I know the way you've treated other guys you've been with,
Luck be a lady with me.

A lady doesn't leave her escort;
It isn't fair,
It isn't nice!
A lady doesn't wander all over the room
And blow on some other guy's dice.

So, let's keep the party polite,
Never get out of my sight.
Stick with me baby I'm the fellow you came in with.
Luck be a lady, luck be a lady,
Luck be a lady tonight.

Make Someone Happy

Words by Betty Comden and Adolph Green
Music by Jule Styne

from *Do Re Mi*

The sound of applause is delicious.
It's a thrill to have the world at your feet.
The praise of the crowd is exciting,
But I've learned that is not what makes a life complete.

There's one thing you can do
For the rest of your days
That's worth more than applause,
The screaming crowd, the bouquets.

Refrain:
Make someone happy.
Make just one someone happy.
Make just one heart the heart you sing to.
One smile that cheers you,
One face that lights when it nears you,
One man you're everything to.

Fame, if you win it,
Comes and goes in a minute.
Where's the real stuff in life to cling to?
Love is the answer,
Someone to love is the answer.
Once you've found him,
Build your world around him.
Make someone happy,
Make just one someone happy,
And you will be happy too.

Makin' Whoopee!

Lyrics by Gus Kahn
Music by Walter Donaldson

from *Whoopee!*

Ev'rytime I hear that march from *Lohengrin,*
I am always on the outside looking in.
Maybe that is why I see the funny side,
When I see a fallen brother take a bride.
Weddings make a lot of people sad.
But if you're not the groom, they're not so
    bad.

Another bride,
Another June,
Another sunny
Honeymoon.
Another season,
Another reason,
For makin' whoopee!

A lot of shoes
A lot of rice,
The groom is nervous
He answers twice.
It's really killing
That he's so willing
To make whoopee!

Picture a little love-nest,
Down where the roses cling.
Picture the same sweet love-nest,
Think what a year can bring.

He's washing dishes,
And baby clothes,
He's so ambitious,
He even sews.

But don't forget folks,
That's what you get, folks,
For makin' whoopee!

Another year,
Or maybe less.
What's this I hear?
Well, can't you guess?
She feels neglected,
And he's suspected,
Of makin' whoopee!

She sits alone,
'Most ev'ry night.
He doesn't phone her,
He doesn't write.
He says he's "busy"
But she says "is he?"
He's makin' whoopee!

He doesn't make much money,
Only five thousand per.
Some judge who thinks he's funny,
Says "you'll pay six to her."

He says, "Now judge,
Suppose I fail?"
The judge says, "Budge
Right into jail."
You'd better keep her,
I think it's cheaper,
Than makin' whoopee!

Mame

Music and Lyric by Jerry Herman

from *Mame*

You coax the blues right out of the horn, Mame,
You charm the husk right off of the corn, Mame.
You've got the banjoes strummin'
And plunkin' out a tune to beat the band,
The whole plantation's hummin'
Since you brought Dixie back to Dixieland.

You make the cotton easy to pick, Mame.
You give my old mint julep a kick, Mame.
You make the old magnolia tree
Blossom at the mention of your name,
You've made us feel alive again,
You've given us the drive again,
To make the South revive again, Mame.

You've brought the cakewalk back into style, Mame.
You make the weepin' willow tree smile, Mame.
Your skin is Dixie satin,
There's rebel in your manner and your speech.
You may be from Manhattan,
But Georgia never had a sweeter peach.

You make our black-eyed peas and our grits, Mame,
Seem like the bill of fare at the Ritz, Mame.
You came, you saw, you conquered
And absolutely nothing is the same.
Your special fascination 'll
Prove to be inspirational,
We think you're just sensational,
Mame.

Many a New Day

Lyrics by Oscar Hammerstein II
Music by Richard Rodgers

from *Oklahoma!*

Why should a womern who is healthy and
  strong
Blubber like a baby if her man goes away?
A-weepin' and a-wailin' how he's done her
  wrong—
That's one thing you'll never hear me say!
Never gonna think that the man I lose
Is the only man among men.
I'll snap my fingers to show I don't care.
I'll buy me a brand-new dress to wear.
I'll scrub my neck and I'll bresh my hair,
And start all over again!

Many a new face will please my eye,
Many a new love will find me.
Never've I once looked back to sigh
Over the romance behind me.
Many a new day will dawn before I do!
Many a light lad may kiss and fly,
A kiss gone by is bygone;
Never've I asked an August sky,
"Where has last July gone?"
Never've I wandered through the rye,
Wonderin' where has some guy gone—
Many a new day will dawn before I do!

Many a new face will please my eye,
Many a new love will find me.
Never've I once looked back to sigh
Over the romance behind me.
Many a new day will dawn before I do!
Never've I chased the honeybee
Who carelessly cajoled me;
Somebody else just as sweet as he
Cheered me and consoled me.
Never've I wept into my tea
Over the deal someone doled me—
Many a new day will dawn,
Many a red sun will set,
Many a blue moon will shine, before I do!

Manhattan

Words by Lorenz Hart
Music by Richard Rodgers

from the Broadway Musical *The Garrick Gaieties*

Verse:
Summer journeys to Niagara
And to other places aggra-
Vate all our cares.
We'll save our fares!
I've a cozy little flat in
What is known as Manhattan,
We'll settle down
Right here in town!

Refrain:
We'll have Manhattan
The Bronx and Staten Island too.
It's lovely going through the zoo.
It's very fancy
On old Delancey Street, you know.
The subway charms us so
When balmy breezes blow
To and fro.
And tell me what street
Compares with Mott Street in July?
Sweet pushcarts gently gliding by.
The great big city's a wondrous toy
Just made for a girl and boy.
We'll turn Manhattan
Into an isle of joy.

We'll go to Greenwich,
Where modern men itch to be free;
And Bowling Green you'll see with me.
We'll bathe at Brighton;
The fish you'll frighten when you're in,
Your bathing suit so thin
Will make the shellfish grin
Fin to fin.
I'd like to take a
Sail on Jamaica Bay with you.
And fair Canarsie's Lake we'll view.
The city's bustle cannot destroy
The dreams of a girl and boy.
We'll turn Manhattan
Into an isle of joy.

We'll go to Yonkers
Where true love conquers in the wilds.
And starve together, dear, in Childs.
We'll go to Coney
And eat baloney on a roll.
In Central Park we'll stroll
Where our first kiss we stole,
Soul to soul.
Our future babies
We'll take to Abie's Irish Rose.
I hope they'll live to see it close.
The city's clamor can never spoil
The dreams of a boy and goil.
We'll turn Manhattan
Into an isle of joy.

We'll have Manhattan,
The Bronx and Staten Island too.
We'll try to cross Fifth Avenue.
As black as onyx
We'll find the Bronnix Park Express.
Our Flatbush flat, I guess,
Will be a great success,
More or less.
A short vacation
On Inspiration Point we'll spend,
And in the station house we'll end.
But Civic Virtue cannot destroy
The dreams of a girl and boy.
We'll turn Manhattan
Into an isle of joy.

Master of the House

Music by Claude-Michel Schönberg
Lyrics by Herbert Kretzmer
Original Text by Alain Boublil and Jean-Marc Natel

from *Les Misérables*

Thernardier:
Welcome, M'sieur.
Sit yourself down,
And meet the best innkeeper in town.
As for the rest,
All of them crooks,
Rooking the guests and cooking the books.
Seldom do you see
Honest men like me.
A gent of good intent
Who's content to be:

Master of the house,
Doling out the charm,
Ready with a handshake and an open palm.
Tells a saucy tale,
Makes a little stir,
Customers appreciate a bon viveur.
Glad to do a friend a favor,
Doesn't cost me to be nice,
But nothing gets you nothing,
Ev'rything has got a little price.

Master of the house,
Keeper of the zoo,
Ready to relieve them of a sou or two.
Watering the wine,
Making up the weight,
Picking up their knickknacks
When they can't see straight.

Ev'rybody loves a landlord.
Ev'rybody's bosom friend.
I do whatever pleases,
Jesus, don't I bleed 'em in the end!
How it all increases,
All them bits and pieces,
Jesus, it's amazing how it grows!

Refrain:
Master of the house,
Quick to catch your eye,
Never wants a passerby to pass him by.
Servant to the poor,
Butler to the great,
Comforter, philosopher and lifelong mate.
Ev'rybody's boon companion,
Ev'rybody's chaperone,
Thernardier:
But lock up your valises,
Jesus, won't I skin you to the bone!

Enter, M'sieur,
Lay down your load,
Unlace your boots and rest from the road.
This weighs a ton.
Travel's a curse.
But here we strive to lighten your purse.
Here the goose is cooked.
Here the fat is fried.
And nothing's overlooked
Till I'm satisfied.

Food beyond compare,
Food beyond belief,
Mix it in a mincer and pretend it's beef.
Kidney of a horse,
Liver of a cat,
Filling up the sausages with this and that.
Residents are more than welcome.
Bridal suite is occupied.
Reasonable charges,
Plus some little extras on the side.

Charge 'em for the lice,
Extra for the mice,
Two percent for looking in the mirror twice.
Here a little slice,
There a little cut,
Three per cent for sleeping with the window
    shut.
When it comes to fixing prices,
There are lots of tricks he knows.
How it all increases,
All them bits and pieces,
Jesus, it's amazing how it grows!

Refrain

Madame Thernardier:
I used to dream that I would meet a prince.
But, God Almighty,
Have you seen what's happened since?

Master of the house?
Isn't worth my spit!
Comforter, philosopher and lifelong shit!
Cunning little brain,
Regular Voltaire.
Thinks he's quite a lover but there's not
    much there!
What a cruel trick of nature
Landed me with such a louse.
God knows how I've lasted
Living with this bastard in the house!

Refrain:
Master of the house,
Master and a half,
Comforter, philosopher—don't make me
    laugh!
Servant to the poor,
Butler to the great,
Hypocrite and toady and inebriate!
Ev'rybody bless our landlord.
Ev'rybody bless his spouse.
Thernardier:
Ev'rybody raise a glass,
Madame Thernardier:
Raise it up the master's ass!
All:
Ev'rybody raise a glass
To the master of the house!

Maybe

Lyric by Martin Charnin
Music by Charles Strouse

from the Musical Production *Annie*

Maybe far away,
Or maybe real nearby,
He may be pouring her coffee,
She may be straightning his tie.
Maybe in a house
All hidden by a hill,
She's sitting playing piano,
He's sitting paying a bill.

Betcha they're young,
Betcha they're smart,
Bet they collect things like ashtrays and art.
Betcha they're good,
(Why shouldn't they be?)
Their one mistake was giving up me.

So maybe now it's time,
And maybe when I wake,
They'll be there calling me "Baby,"
Maybe.

Betcha he reads,
Betcha she sews,
Maybe she's made me a closet of clothes.
Maybe they're strict.
As straight as a line,
Don't really care as long as they're mine.

So, maybe now this prayer's
The last one of its kind;
Won't you please come get your "baby?"
Maybe.

Maybe This Time

Words by Fred Ebb
Music by John Kander

from the Musical *Cabaret*

Maybe this time,
I'll be lucky.
Maybe this time he'll stay.
Maybe this time,
For the first time,
Love won't hurry away.
He will hold me fast.
I'll be home at last.
Not a loser anymore,
Like the last time and the time before.

Everybody
Loves a winner
So nobody loved me.
Lady Peaceful.
Lady Happy

That's what I long to be.
All the odds are
In my favor
Something's bound to begin.
It's got to happen,
Happen sometime;
Maybe this time I'll win.

Repeat Verse 2

Miss Marmelstein

Words and Music by Harold Rome

from *I Can Get It for You Wholesale*

Refrain:
Why is it always Miss Marmelstein?
(Miss Marmelstein!)
Miss Marmelstein?
(Miss Marmelstein!)
Oh, Miss Marmelstein?
(Miss Marmelstein!)

Other girls they call
By their first names right away.
They get cozy, intimay.
Know what I mean?
Nobody calls me, hey, Baby Doll,
(Miss Marmelstein!)
Or Honey Dear,
(Miss Marmelstein!)
Or Sweetie Pie.
(Miss Marmelstein!)

Even my first name would be preferable,
Though it's turrible,
It might be better,
It's Yetta.
Or perhaps my second name,
That's Tessye,
Spelled T—E—S—S—Y—
E!

But no, no, it's always Miss Marmelstein.
(Miss Marmelstein!)
You'd think at least Miss M.,
They could try.

(Miss Marmelstein!)
Miss Marmelstein!
(Miss Marmelstein!)
Miss Marmelstein!
(Miss Marmelstein!)
Oh, I could die!

I'm a very willing secretary.
Enjoy my work,
As my employer will corroborate.
Except for one disappointment,
One fly in the ointment,
It's great, I mean, simply great!

The aggravation of my situation,
I might as well get it off my chest,
Is the drab appellation,
Spoken:
(Pardon the big words I apply,
But I was an English major at C.C.N.Y.)
Sung:
The drab appellation,
With which I am persistently addressed,
Persistently, perpetually,
Continually, inevitably addressed!
Spoken:
Believe me, it could drive a person
Positively psychosomatic!

Refrain

Other girls get called
By their nicknames right away,
Slightly naughty or risqué,
Know what I mean?
Nobody calls me, Hey, Cooch-y-coo,
(Miss Marmelstein!)
Or Boobaleh,
(Miss Marmelstein!)
Or Passion Pie!
(Miss Marmelstein!)

Even, "Hey there, babe,"
Though not respectable,
Ain't so objectable.
It's kind of crummy, but chummy.
'Course, if I got married,
That would do it.
So where's the lucky guy?
(Huh!)

Till then, it still is Miss Marmelstein.
(Miss Marmelstein!)
Ev'ry day I get more and more fussed.
(Miss Marmelstein!)
Miss Marmelstein!
(Miss Marmelstein!)
Miss Marmelstein!
(Miss Marmelstein!)
Oh, I,
I could bust!

Mountain Greenery

Words by Lorenz Hart
Music by Richard Rodgers

from the Broadway Musical *The Garrick Gaieties*

He:
On the first of May
It is moving day;
Spring is here, so blow your job,
Throw jour job away;
Now's the time to trust
To your wanderlust.
In the city's dust you wait,
Must you wait?
Just you wait:

In a mountain greenery,
Where God paints the scenery,
Just two crazy people together;
While you love your lover,
Let blue skies be your coverlet,
When it rains we'll laugh at the weather.
And if you're good
I'll search for wood,
So you can cook
While I stand looking.
Beans could get no keener reception in a
    beanery,
Bless our mountain greenery home!

She:
Simple cooking means
More than French cuisines.
I've a banquet planned
Which is sandwiches and beans,
Coffee's just as grand
With a little sand.
Eat and you'll grow fatter, boy,
S'matter, boy?
'Atta boy!

In a mountain greenery,
Where God paints the scenery,
Just two crazy people together;
How we love sequestering
Where no pests are pestering,
No dear mama holds us in tether!
Mosquitoes here
Won't bite you, dear;
I'll let them sting
Me on the finger.
We could find no cleaner retreat from life's
    machinery
Than our mountain greenery home!

He:
When the world was young,
Old Father Adam with sin would grapple,
So we're entitled to just one apple,
I mean to make applesauce.

She:
Underneath the bough,
We'll learn a lesson from Mister Omar;
Beneath the eyes of no Pa and no Ma,
Old Lady Nature is boss.

He:
Washing dishes,
Catching fishes
In the running stream,
We'll curse the smell o'
Citronella,
Even when we dream.

She:
Head upon the ground,
Your downy pillow is just a boulder.
He:
I'll have new dimples before I'm older;
But life is peaches and cream.

And if you're good,
I'll search for wood,
So you can cook.
While I stand looking.
Both:
Beans could get no keener reception in a
    beanery.
Bless our mountain greenery home.

Mutual Admiration Society

Words by Matt Dubey
Music by Harold Karr

from *Happy Hunting*

Refrain:
We belong to a mutual admiration society,
My baby and me.
We belong to a mutual admiration society!

She thinks I'm handsome and I'm smart,
I think that she's a work of art.
She says that I'm the greatest man,
And likewise, I'm her biggest fan.
I say her kisses are like wine,
She says they're not as good as mine,
And that's the way we pass the time of day!
My baby and me,
Oh, we belong to a mutual admiration
    society!

Refrain

She says, "Oh, you're the sweetest one,"
I say, "No, you're the sweetest one."
She claims that I'm a nat'ral wit,
I say it's just the opposite.
The only fightin' that we do
Is just who loves who more than who,
And we go on like that from night 'til dawn!
My baby and me,
Oh, we belong to a mutual admiration
    society!

Now, I do not exaggerate,
I think she's nothin' short of great.
She says, "That kind of flattery
Will get you any place with me."
The way we carry on,
It tends to just embarrass all our friends,
And that is how we'll still be years from now!
My baby and me,
Oh, we belong to a mutual admiration
    society!
My baby and me!

My Cup Runneth Over

Words by Tom Jones
Music by Harvey Schmidt

from *I Do! I Do!*

Girl:
Sometimes in the morning, when shadows are deep,
I lie here beside you just watching you sleep.
And sometimes I whisper what I'm thinking of,
My cup runneth over with love.

Boy:
Sometimes in the evening, when you do not see,
I study the small things you do constantly.
I memorize moments that I'm fondest of.
My cup runneth over with love.

Both:
In only a moment we both will be old.
We won't even notice the world turning cold.
And so, in this moment, with sunlight above,
My cup runneth over with love.

Boy: With love,
Girl: With love.

My Defenses Are Down

Words and Music by Irving Berlin

from the Stage Production *Annie Get Your Gun*

I had my way with so many girls,
And it was lots of fun,
My system was to know many girls,
'Twould keep me safe from one.
I find it can't be done.

My defenses are down,
She's broken my resistance
And I don't know where I am.
I went into the fight like a lion,
But I came out like a lamb.

My defenses are down,
She's got me where she wants me
And I can't escape no-how.
I could speak to my heart when it weakened,
But my heart won't listen now.

Like a toothless, clawless tiger,
Like an organ grinder's bear,
Like a knight without his armor,
Like Samson without his hair.

My defenses are down,
I might as well surrender,
For the battle can't be won.
But, I must confess that I like it,
So there's nothing to be done,
Yes, I must confess that I like it,
Being mis'rable is gonna be fun.

My Favorite Things

Lyrics by Oscar Hammerstein II
Music by Richard Rodgers

from *The Sound of Music*

Raindrops on roses and whiskers on kittens.
Bright copper kettles and warm woolen mittens.
Brown paper packages tied up with strings,
These are a few of my favorite things.

Cream-colored ponies and crisp apple strudels,
Doorbells and sleigh-bells and schnitzel with noodles,
Wild geese that fly with the moon on their wings,
These are a few of my favorite things.

Girls in white dresses with blue satin sashes,
Snowflakes that stay on my nose and eyelashes,
Silver white winters that melt into springs,
These are a few of my favorites things.

When the dog bites,
When the bees stings,
When I'm feeling sad,
I simply remember my favorite things
And then I don't feel so bad!

My Funny Valentine

Words by Lorenz Hart
Music by Richard Rodgers

from *Babes in Arms*

Behold the way our fine-feathered friend
His virtue doth parade.
Though knowest not, my dim-witted friend,
The picture thou hast made.
Thy vacant brow and thy tousled hair
Conceal thy good intent.
Thou noble, upright, truthful, sincere,
And slightly dopey gent, you're…

My funny Valentine,
Sweet comic Valentine,
You make me smile with my heart.
Your looks are laughable,
Unphotographable,
Yet you're my favorite work of art.
Is your figure less than Greek?
Is your mouth a little weak?
When you open it to speak
Are you smart?
But don't change a hair for me,
Not if you care for me,
Stay, little Valentine, stay!
Each day is Valentine's Day.

My Time of Day

By Frank Loesser

from *Guys and Dolls*

My time of day is the dark-time,
A couple of deals before dawn,
When the street belongs to the cop,
And the janitor with the mop,
And the grocery clerks are all gone.
When the smell of the rain-washed pavement
Comes up clean and fresh and cold,
And the street lamplight
Fills the gutter with gold,
That's my time of day,
My time of day,
And you're the only doll I've ever wanted,
To share it with me.

A New Life

Words by Leslie Bricusse
Music by Frank Wildhorn

from *Jekyll & Hyde*

A new life,
What I wouldn't give to have a new life!
One thing I learned as I go through life,
Nothing is for free along the way!

A new start,
That's the thing I need to give me new heart.
Half a chance in life to find a new part,
Just a simple role that I can play.

A new hope,
Something to convince me to renew hope!
A new day,
Bright enough to help me find my way!
A new chance,
One that maybe has a touch of romance.
Where can it be?
The chance for me?

A new dream,
I have one I know that very few dream!
I would like to see that overdue dream,
Even though it never may come true!

A new love,
Though I know there's no such thing as true
    love.
Even so, although I never knew love,
Still I feel that one dream is my due!

A new world,
This one thing I want to ask of you, world.
Once! Before it's time to bid adieu, world!
One sweet chance to prove the cynics wrong!

A new life,
More and more I'm sure, as I go through
    life,
Just to play the game and to pursue life,
Just to share its pleasures and belong!
That's what I've been here for all along!
Each day's a brand new life!

No Other Love

Lyrics by Oscar Hammerstein II
Music by Richard Rodgers

from *Me and Juliet*

No other love have I,
Only my love for you,
Only the dream we knew,
No other love.

Watching the night go by,
Wishing that you could be
Watching the night with me,
Into the night I cry:
Hurry home, come home to me!
Set me free,
Free from doubt,
And free from longing.

Into your arms I'll fly.
Locked in your arms I'll stay,
Waiting to hear you say:
No other love have I,
No other love.

Nobody's Chasing Me

Words and Music by Cole Porter

from *Out of This World*

The breeze is chasing the zephyr,
The moon is chasing the sea,
The bull is chasing the heifer,
But nobody's chasing me.
The cock is chasing the chicken,
The peewee, some wee peewee,
The cat is taking a lickin',
But nobody's taking me.

Nobody wants to own me,
And I object.
Nobody wants to phone me,
Even collect.

The leopard's chasing the leopard,
The chimp, some champ chimpanzee,
The sheep is chasing the shepherd,
But nobody's chasing me,
Nobody,
Nobody's chasing me.

The flood is chasing the levee,
The wolf is out on a spree,
The Ford is chasing the Chevvy,
But nobody's chasing me.
The snake with passion is shakin'
The pooch is chasing the flea,
The moose, his love-call is making,
But nobody's chasing me.

Each night I get the mirror
From off the shelf.
Each night I'm getting nearer,
Chasing myself.

The clams are almost amixin',
The hams are chasing T.V.,
The fox is chasing the vixen,
But nobody's chasing me.
Nobody,
Nobody's chasing me.

ADDITIONAL LYRICS
Refrain 2:
The flood is chasing the levee,
The wolf is out on a spree,
The Ford is chasing the Chevvy,
But nobody's chasing me.
The bee is chasing Hymettus,
The queen is chasing the bee,
The worm is chasing the lettuce,
But nobody's chasing me.

Each night I get the mirror
From off the shelf.
Each night I'm getting queerer,
Chasing myself.

Ravel is chasing Debussy,
The aphis chases the pea,
The gander's chasing the goosey,
But nobody's goosing me.
Nobody,
Nobody's chasing me.

Refrain 3:
The rain's pursuing the roses,
The snow, the trim Christmas tree,
Big dough pursues Grandma Moses,
But no one's pursuing me.
While Isis chases Osiris,
And Pluto, Proserpine,
My doc is chasing my virus,
But nobody's chasing me.

I'd like to learn canasta,
Yet how can I?
What wife without her masta
Can multiply?

The clams are almost a-mixin',
The hams are chasing T.V.,
The fox is chasing the vixen,
But nobody's vixin' me.
Nobody,
Nobody's chasing me.

Refrain 4:
The llama's chasing the llama,
Papa is chasing Mama,
Monsieur is chasing Madame,
But nobody's chasing moi.
The dove, each moment, is bolda,
The lark sings "Ich liebe dich,"
Tristan is chasing Isolda,
But nobody's chasing mich.

Although I may be Juno,
B'lieve it or not,
I've got a lot of you-know,
And you know what!

The snake with passion is shakin',
The pooch is chasing the flea,
The moose his love call is makin',
[Sung with head cold]
But dobody's baki'd be.
Dobody *(sneeze)*,
Nobody's chasing me.

Nobody's Heart

Words by Lorenz Hart
Music by Richard Rodgers

from *By Jupiter*

Refrain:
Nobody's heart belongs to me,
Heigh-ho!
Who cares?
Nobody writes his songs to me,
No one belongs to me,
That's the least of my cares.

I may be sad at times,
And disinclined to play,
But, it's not bad at times,
To go your own sweet way.

Nobody's arms belong to me,
No arms feel strong to me,
I admire the moon,
As a moon,
Just a moon,
Nobody's heart belongs to me today.

Refrain

Ride, Amazon ride.
Hunt your stags and bears.
Take life in its stride.
Heigh-ho!
Who cares?
Go hunting with pride,
Track bears to their lairs.
Ride, Amazon ride!
Heigh-ho,
Who cares?

Refrain

Nothing Can Stop Me Now!

Words and Music by Leslie Bricusse and Anthony Newley

from *The Roar of the Greasepaint—The Smell of the Crowd*

I don't believe it,
Pinch me to see if I am awake.
I can't believe it,
Wake me and say there's been a mistake.
No don't!
I'd sooner sleep on,
In case, that is,
Until the dream has gone.
No, this is no dream, my friend.
This, it would seem,
Is where my troubles end.

Stand well back, I'm coming through,
Nothing can stop me now.
Watch out, world, I'm warning you,
Nothing can stop me now.

Now I know that there is a promised land,
I'm gonna find it, and how.
Hope is high and I'm gonna cling to it,
Tie ev'ry string to it,
Give ev'rything to it.

I'll make all my dreams come true
Before my final bow.
How I'll do it, who can say?
But I know I will some day.
Watch out, world, I'm on my way,
Nothing can stop me now.

I shall find success today,
Nothing can stop me now.
Yesterday was yesterday,
Nothing can stop me now.

Now I know the future is mine to have,
I'm hereby making a vow.
From now on I'm gonna begin again,
Stick out my chin again,
Go in and win again.

Get you gone, you sky of grey.
Farewell you furrowed brow.
Now my future's crystal clear.
No more woe for me to fear.
I'm gonna stand this world upon its ear,
And I'll succeed somehow,
Nothing can stop me now.

Oh, What a Beautiful Mornin'

Lyrics by Oscar Hammerstein II
Music by Richard Rodgers

from *Oklahoma!*

There's a bright golden haze on the meadow,
There's a bright golden haze on the meadow.
The corn is as high as an elephant's eye,
An' it looks like it's climbin' clear up to the sky.

Refrain:
Oh, what a beautiful mornin'!
Oh, what a beautiful day!
I got a beautiful feelin'
Everything's goin' my way.

All the cattle are standin' like statues,
All the cattle are standin' like statues.
They don't turn their heads as they see me ride by,
But a little brown maverick is winkin' her eye.

Refrain

All the sounds of the earth are like music,
All the sounds of the earth are like music.
The breeze is so busy it don't miss a tree,
And a ol' weepin' willer is laughin' at me.

Refrain

Oh, what a beautiful day!

Oklahoma

Lyrics by Oscar Hammerstein II
Music by Richard Rodgers

from *Oklahoma!*

They couldn't pick a better time to start in life,
It ain't too early and it ain't too late.
Startin' as a farmer with a brand-new wife—
Soon be livin' in a brand-new state!
Brand-new state
Gonna treat you great!

Gonna give you barley,
Carrots and pertaters—
Pasture fer the cattle—
Spinach and termayters!
Flowers on the prairie where the June bugs zoom—
Plen'y of air and plen'y of room—
Plen'y of room to swing a rope,
Plen'y of heart and plen'y of hope.

Oklahoma,
Where the wind comes sweepin' down the plain
(And the wavin' wheat
Can sure smell sweet
When the wind comes right behind the rain)
Oklahoma!
Every night my honey lamb and I
Sit alone and talk
And watch a hawk
Makin' lazy circles in the sky.
We know we belong to the land,
And the land we belong to is grand.
And when we say:
Ee-ee-ow! A-yip-i-o-ee-ay!
We're only sayin',
You're doin' fine, Oklahoma!
Oklahoma, O.K.!

Old Devil Moon

Words by E.Y. Harburg
Music by Burton Lane

from *Finian's Rainbow*

I look at you and suddenly,
Something in your eyes I see
Soon begins bewitchin' me.
It's that old devil moon
That you stole from the skies.
It's that old devil moon in your eyes.

You and your glance
Make this romance
Too hot to handle,
Stars in the night,
Blazing their light
Can't hold a candle
To your razzle dazzle.

You've got me flyin' high and wide
On a magic carpet ride,
Full of butterflies inside.
Wanna cry, wanna croon,
Wanna laugh like a loon.

It's that old devil moon in your eyes.
Just when I think I'm free as a dove,
Old devil moon, deep in your eyes,
Blinds me with love.

An Old Man

Lyrics by Martin Charnin
Music by Richard Rodgers

from *Two by Two*

An old man is queer in his ways,
His appetite fails,
But he's hungry for praise.
And the sights that he's seen
Cloud the sights that he'll see.
Old isn't easy to be.

An old man gets cranky at night,
When barrels won't lift
And an apple won't bite.
When what used to be sure
Has a whole other face,
Old is an unfriendly place.

He walks like he's smoothing out bumps in a
    rug,
For hours he'll stare at a spot.
The hug that he gives you is hardly a hug,
You remember the hug that it's not anymore.

An old man, he's sometimes afraid;
He sings to the sun,
But he's partial to shade.
To himself, he's a wit,
To the world he's a pest!
Old isn't what he does best.

An old man, he shivers in bed,
It's all of the years
That have spun 'round his head.
He's the burdensome thing
That a fam'ly ignores.
He's to put in a room
And to lock all the doors—
Except—
Except—
Except when an old man is yours.

Once in Love with Amy

By Frank Loesser

from *Where's Charley?*

I caught you, sir,
Having a look at her,
As she went strolling by.
Now, didn't your heart go boom,
Boom, boom, boom, boom?
Now didn't you hear a sigh?

I warn you, sir,
Don't start to dream of her,
Just bid such thoughts be gone,
Or it will be boom, boom,
Boom, boom, boom, boom,
Boom, boom, boom, boom, boom,
From then on.

For, once in love with Amy,
Always in love with Amy,
Ever and ever fascinated by her,
Sets your heart afire to stay.

Once you're kiss'd by Amy,
Tear up your list, it's Amy,
Ply her with bonbons, poetry and flowers,
Moon a million hours away.

You might be quite the fickle hearted rover,
So carefree, and bold,
Who loves a girl, and later thinks it over,
And just quits cold.

Ah, but once in love with Amy,
Always in love with Amy,
Ever and ever,
Sweetly you'll romance her,
Trouble is, the answer will be,
(Laughs) Ha, ha, ha, ha,
That Amy'd rather stay in love with me!

Once Upon a Dream

Words by Steve Cuden, Leslie Bricusse and Frank Wildhorn
Music by Frank Wildhorn

from *Jekyll & Hyde*

When this all began,
I knew there'd be a price.

Once upon a dream,
I was lost in love's embrace.
There I found a perfect place,
Once upon a dream.

Once there was a time
Like no other time before,
Hope was still an open door,
Once upon a dream.

And I was unafraid,
The dream was so exciting!
But now I see it fade,
And I am here alone!

Once upon a dream,
You were heaven sent to me,
Was it never meant to be?
Are you just a dream?
Could we begin again,
Once upon a dream?

Once You Lose Your Heart

Words and Music by Noel Gay

from *Me and My Girl*

Once you lose your heart,
Once somebody takes it,
From the place it rested in before.
Once you lose your heart,
Once somebody wakes it,
Then it isn't your heart any more.

Refrain:
It's gone before you knew
It could ever go that way,
And now you must pursue it,
Forever and a day.

Once you lose your heart,
Once somebody takes it,
There's one thing certain from the start,
You'll find forever,
You've got to follow your heart.

They say a girl should never be without love,
And all the joy that love alone can bring.
All that I have ever learnt about love,
Tells me it's a very funny thing.
For when your heart is fancy-free,
You hope some man will choose it,
But oh, the spin you'll find you're in,
The very moment that you lose it.

Once you lose your heart,
Once somebody takes it,
From the place it rested in before.
Once you lose your heart,
Once somebody takes it,
Then it isn't your heart any more.

Refrain

Once you lose your heart,
Once somebody takes it,
There's one thing certain from the start,
You've got to follow,
You've got to follow your heart.

One

Music by Marvin Hamlisch
Lyric by Edward Kleban

from *A Chorus Line*

One
Singular sensation
Every step that she takes.
One
Thrilling combination
Every move that she makes.
One smile and suddenly nobody else will do.
You know you'll never be lonely with you-know-who.

One
Moment in her presence
And you can forget the rest.
For the girl is second best to none, son.
Ooh! Sigh!
Give her your attention,
Do I really have to mention
She's the one?

One Song Glory

Words and Music by Jonathan Larson

from *Rent*

One song glory.
One song before I go.
Glory,
One song to leave behind.
Find one song,
One last refrain.
Glory from the pretty boy front man,
Who wasted opportunity.
One song,
He had the world at his feet.
Glory in the eyes of a young girl,
A young girl.
Find glory beyond the cheap colored lights,
One song before the sun sets,
Glory on another empty life.
Time flies,
Time dies.

Glory,
One blaze of glory,
One blaze of glory.
Glory.
Find glory in a song that rings true,
Truth like a blazing fire,
An eternal flame.
Find one song,
A song about love.
Glory from the soul of a young man,
A young man.

Find the one song,
Before the virus takes hold,
Glory like a sunset.
One song to redeem this empty life.
Time flies,
And then no need to endure anymore.
Time dies.

Our Language of Love

Music by Marguerite Monnot
Original French Words by Alexandre Breffort
English Words by Julian More, David Heneker and Monty Norman

from *Irma La Douce*

No need to speak,
No need to sing,
When just a glance means ev'rything.
Not a word need be spoken,
In our language of love.

I'll touch your cheek,
You'll hold my hand,
And only we will understand
That the silence is broken,
By our language of love.

It's clear to you,
It's clear to me,
This precious moment had to be,
Other moments outclassing,
Guardian angels are passing.

No words will do,
No lips can say
The tender meaning we convey,
"I love you" is unspoken,
In our language of love.

The Party's Over

Words by Betty Comden and Adolph Green
Music by Jule Styne

from *Bells Are Ringing*

The party's over,
It's time to call it a day.
They've burst your pretty balloon
And taken the moon away.
It's time to wind up
The masquerade.
Just make your mind up
The piper must be paid.

The party's over,
The candles flicker and dim.
You danced and dreamed through the night,
It seemed to be right,
Just being with him.
Now you must wake up,
All dreams must end.
Take off your make-up,
The party's over,
It's all over,
My friend.

Red, Hot and Blue

Words and Music by Cole Porter

from *Red, Hot and Blue!*

Due to the tragic lowness of my brow,
All music that's high brow,
Gets me upset.
Each time I hear a strain of Stravinsky's,
I hurry to Minsky's,
And try to forget.
I don't like Schubert's music or Schumann's,
I'm one of those humans
Who only goes in for Berlin and Vincent Youmans;
I'm for the guy that eludes
Bach sonatas and Chopin preludes,
So when some nice man I meet,
I always murmur tout d'suite.

Refrain:
If you want to thrill me,
And drill me for your crew,
Sing me a melody that's red, hot and blue.
Before you expand
On that grand cottage for two,
Sing me a melody that's red, hot and blue.

I can't take Sibelius or Delius,
But I swear I'd throw my best pal away
For Calloway.

So when we're all set and I get married to you,
Don't let that violin
Start playing *Lohengrin*,
It may be sweet as sin,
But it's not red, hot and blue.

Refrain

Ribbons Down My Back

Music and Lyric by Jerry Herman

from *Hello, Dolly!*

I'll be wearing ribbons down my back,
This summer.
Blue and green, and streaming in the yellow sky.
So if someone special comes my way,
This summer,
He might notice me passing by.

And so I'll try to make it easier to find me,
In the stillness of July,
Because a breeze might stir a rainbow up behind me
That might happen to catch the gentleman's eye.

And he might smile and take me by the hand,
This summer,
Making me recall how lovely love can be.
And so I will proudly wear ribbons down my back,
Shining in my hair,
That he might notice me.

River in the Rain

Words and Music by Roger Miller

from *Big River*

Refrain 1:
River in the rain,
Sometimes at night you look like a long white train,
Windin' your way, away somewhere.
River, I love you,
Don't you care?

If you're on the run,
Windin' someplace just tryin' to find the sun.
Whether the sunshine, whether the rain,
River, I love you, just the same.

Refrain 2:
But sometimes in a time of trouble,
When you're out of hand and your muddy bubbles
Roll across my floor,
Carryin' way the things I treasure;
Hell, there ain't no way to measure
Why I love you more
Than I did the day before.

Refrain 1

Refrain 2

River in the rain,
Sometimes at night you look like a long white train,
Windin' your way away from me.
River, I've never seen the sea.

Ridin' High

Words and Music by Cole Porter

from *Red, Hot and Blue!*

Love had socked me,
Simply knocked me for a loop.
Luck has dished me,
Till you fished me from the soup.
Now together,
We can weather anything.
So, please, don't sputter,
If I should mutter.

Life's great, life's grand,
Future all planned.
No more clouds in the sky,
How'm I ridin'?
I'm ridin' high.

Someone I love,
Mad for my love,
So long Jonah, goodbye.
How'm I ridin'?
I'm ridin' high.

Floating on a starlit ceiling,
Doting on the cards I'm dealing,
Gloating, because I'm feeling so hap-hap-
   happy,
I'm slap happy.

So ring bells, sing songs,
Blow horns, beat gongs,
Our love never will die,
How'm I ridin'?
I'm ridin' high.

ADDITIONAL LYRICS
Patter:
What do I care if Missus Harrison Williams
Is the best dressed woman in town?
What do I care if Countess Barbara Hutton
Has a Rolls-Royce built for each gown?
Why should I have the vapors
When I read in the papers
That Missus Simpson dined behind the
   throne?
I've got a cute king of my own.

What do I care if Katie Hepburn
Is famous for the world's most beautiful
   nose,
Or, if I, for my sins,
Don't possess underpins
Like the pegs "Legs" Dietrich shows?
I'm feeling swell,
In fact so well
It's time some noise began,
For although I'm not a big shot,
Still, I've got my man.

Second Patter:
What do I care if Missus Dorothy Parker,
Has the country's wittiest brain.
What do I care if little Eleanor Jarett
Only swims in vintage champagne?
Why should I be a-flutter
When Republicans mutter
That Missus R. gets pay to write her day,
If I could write my nights, hey, hey!

What do I care if fair Tallulah
Possesses tons and tons of jewels from gents?
Or, if some one observes
That I haven't the curves
That Simone Simon presents?
I'm doin' fine,
My life's divine,
I'm living in the sun,
'Cause I've a big date
With my fate,
So I rate A-1.

The Road You Didn't Take

Words and Music by Stephen Sondheim

from *Follies*

You're either a poet or you're a lover,
Or you're the famous Benjamin Stone.
You take one road,
You try one door,
There isn't time for any more.
One's life consists of either/or.
One has regrets which one forgets,
And as the years go on,

The road you didn't take hardly comes to
    mind,
Does it?
The door you didn't try,
Where could it have led?
The choice you didn't make never was
    defined,
Was it?
Dreams you didn't dare are dead.
Were they ever there?
Who said?
I don't remember,
I don't remember at all.

The books I'll never read wouldn't change a
    thing,
Would they?
The girls I'll never know,
I'm too tired for.
The lives I'll never lead couldn't make me
    sing,
Could they?
Could they?
Could they?

Chances that you miss,
Ignore.
Ignorance is bliss;
What's more, you won't remember,
You won't remember at all,
Not at all.

You yearn for the women,
Long for the money,
Envy the famous Benjamin Stones.
You take your road,
The decades fly,
The yearnings fade, the longings die.
You learn to bid them all goodbye.
And oh, the peace, the blessed peace.
At last you come to know.

The roads you never take go through rocky
    ground,
Don't they?
The choices that you make aren't all that
    grim.
The worlds you never see still will be
    around,
Won't they?
The Ben I'll never be,
Who remembers him?

Seasons of Love

Words and Music by Jonathan Larson

from *Rent*

Five hundred twenty-five thousand
   six hundred minutes,
Five hundred twenty-five thousand
   moments so dear.
Five hundred twenty-five thousand
   six hundred minutes.
How do you measure, measure a year?

In daylights, in sunsets,
In midnights, in cups of coffee,
In inches, in miles, in laughter, in strife,
In five hundred twenty-five thousand
   six hundred minutes.
How do you measure a year in the life.

How about love?
How about love?
How about love?
Measure in love.
Seasons of love,
Seasons of love.

Five hundred twenty-five thousand
   six hundred minutes,
Five hundred twenty-five thousand
   journeys to plan.
Five hundred twenty-five thousand
   six hundred minutes.
How do you measure the life of a woman or
   a man?

In truth that she learned,
Or in times that he cried,
In bridges he burned,
Or the way that she died.
It's time now to sing out,
Though the story never ends.
Let's celebrate, remember,
A year in the life of friends.

Remember the love,
Remember the love,
Remember the love,
Measure in love,
Seasons of love,
Seasons of love.

Satin and Silk

Words and Music by Cole Porter

from *Silk Stockings*

Since my trips have been extensive
  ev'rywhere,
I've become a much wiser gal.
For I've noticed that expensive underwear
Can improve a gal's morale.

It is strange how lovely lingerie
Can affect a gal's false modesty,
If she's wearing silk and satin,
Satin and silk.

Though she knows that boys are evil imps,
Yet she yearns to give those boys a glimpse,
If she's wearing silk and satin,
Satin and silk.

You cannot expect a lady
To exert that certain pull,
If she's wearing flannel bloomers
And her stockings are made of wool.

But a woman's woes are at an end,
And she's all prepared to "make" a friend,
If she's wearing silk and satin,
She's for pettin' and for pattin',
If she's wearing silk and satin,
Satin and silk.

It is strange what undergarments do
To convert a maiden's point of view,
If she's wearing silk and satin,
Satin and silk.

She will never say her pride was hurt,
Should a breeze blow by and lift her skirt,
If she's wearing silk and satin,
Satin and silk.

You cannot expect a debutante
To know she's full of pep,
If her slip is made of cotton
And her panties are made of rep.

But she feels much more self confident,
And will dine alone with any gent,
If she's wearing silk and satin,
Give her broccoli au gratin,
If she's wearing silk and satin,
Satin and silk.

Though a gal may have been born a prude,
She can quite reverse her attitude,
If she's wearing silk and satin,
Satin and silk.

With attractive trimmin's 'neath her dress,
She can shake like hell and spell success,
If she's wearing silk and satin,
Satin and silk.

You cannot expect a burlesque queen
To cherish further hope,
If her bra is made of buckram
And her G-string is made of rope.

But she knows, 'cause she has traveled miles,
She can always lay 'em in the aisles,
If she's wearing silk and satin,
She can flatten Lord Mountbatten
If she's wearing silk and satin,
Satin and silk.

Second Hand Rose

Words by Grant Clarke
Music by James F. Hanley

from *Ziegfeld Follies of 1921*

Verse:
Father has a business,
Strictly second hand,
Everything from toothpicks
To a baby grand.
Stuff in our apartment
Came from father's store.
Even clothes I'm wearing,
Someone wore before.
It's no wonder
That I feel abused.
I never get a thing
That ain't been used.

I'm wearing second hand hats, second hand
  clothes,
That's why they call me second hand Rose.
Even our piano in the parlor,
Father bought for ten cents on the dollar.
Second hand pearls,
I'm wearing second hand curls.
I never get a single thing that's new.
Even Jake the plumber, he's the man I adore,
Had the nerve to tell me he's been married
  before.
Everyone knows that I'm just second hand
  Rose,
From Second Avenue.

I'm wearing second hand shoes, second
  hand hose,
All the girls hand me their second hand
  beaux.
Even my pajamas when I don 'em
Have somebody else's initials on 'em.
Second hand rings, I'm sick of second hand
  things.
I never get what other girlies do.
Once while strolling through the Ritz
A girl got my goat,
She nudged her friend and said,
"Ooh look, here's my old fur coat."
Everyone knows that I'm just Second Hand
  Rose,
From Second Avenue.

September Song

Words by Maxwell Anderson
Music by Kurt Weill

from the Musical Play *Knickerbocker Holiday*

Male:

When I was a young man courting the girls,
I played me a waiting game;
If a maid refused me with tossing curls,
I let the old earth take a couple of whirls,
While I plied her with tears in lieu of pearls
And as time came around she came my way,
As time came around she came.

Refrain:

Oh, it's a long, long while
From May to December,
But the days grow short
When you reach September.
When the autumn weather
Turns the leaves to flame,
One hasn't got time for the waiting game.
Oh, the days dwindle down
To a precious few,
September, November!
And these precious days
I'll spend with you,
These precious days
I'll spend with you.

Female:

When you meet with the young men early in spring,
They court you in song and rhyme,
They woo you with words and clover ring,
But if you examine the goods they bring,
They have little to offer but the songs they sing
And a plentiful waste of time of day,
A plentiful waste of time.

Refrain

Seventy Six Trombones

By Meredith Willson

from Meredith Willson's *The Music Man*

Seventy six trombones led the big parade,
With a hundred and ten cornets close at hand.
They were followed by rows and rows of the finest virtuosos,
The cream of ev'ry famous band.

Seventy six trombones caught the morning sun,
With a hundred and ten cornets right behind.
There were more than a thousand reeds springing up like weeds,
There were horns of ev'ry shape and kind.

There were copper bottom timpani in horse platoons,
Thundering, thundering, all along the way.
Double bell euphoniums and big bassoons,
Each bassoon having his big fat say.
There were fifty mounted cannon in the battery,
Thundering, thundering, louder than before.
Clarinets of ev'ry size and trumpeters who'd improvise
A full octave higher than the score.

Seventy six trombones hit the counterpoint,
While a hundred and ten cornets blazed away.
To the rhythm of Harch! Harch! Harch!
All the kids began to march,
And they're marching still right today.

Shall We Dance?

Lyrics by Oscar Hammerstein II
Music by Richard Rodgers

from *The King and I*

We've just been introduced,
I do not know you well,
But when the music started,
Something drew me to your side.
So many men and girls are in each other's arms—
It made me think we might be
Similarly occupied.

Refrain:
Shall we dance?
On a bright cloud of music shall we fly?
Shall we dance?
Shall we then say "Good night" and mean "Good bye"?
Or, perchance,
When the last little star has left the sky,
Shall we still be together
With our arms around each other
And shall you be my new romance?
On the clear understanding
That this kind of thing can happen,
Shall we dance?
Shall we dance?
Shall we dance?

Shy

Words by Marshall Barer
Music by Mary Rodgers

from *Once Upon a Mattress*

Someone's being bashful.
That's no way to be,
Not with me.
Can't you see
That I am just as embarrassed as you?
And I can understand your point of view.

I've always been shy,
I confess it, I'm shy!
Can't you guess that this confident air
Is a mask that I wear,
'Cause I'm shy?
And you may be sure,
Way down deep I'm demure.
Though some people I know might deny it,
At bottom I'm quiet and pure!

I'm aware that it's wrong to be meek
    as I am,
My chances may pass me by.
I pretend to be strong, but as weak as I am,
All I can do is try.

God knows I try!
Though I'm frightened and shy,
And despite the impression I give,
I confess that I'm living a lie,
Because I'm actually terribly timid,
And horribly shy.

Though a lady may be dripping
    with glamour,
As often as not she'll stumble and stammer,
When suddenly confronted with romance.
And she's likely to fall on her face,
When she's finally face to face
With a pair of pants.

Quite often the lady's not as hard to please
As she seems.
Quite often she'll settle for something less
Than the man of her dreams.

I'm going fishing for a mate.
I'm gonna look in ev'ry nook.
But how much longer must I wait
With baited breath and hook?

And that is why,
Though I'm painfully shy,
I'm insane to know:
Which sir?
You, sir.
Not you, sir.
Then who, sir?
Where, sir,
And when, sir?
I couldn't be tenser,
So let's get this done, man.
Get on with the fun, man.
I am one man shy.

The Simple Joys of Maidenhood

Words by Alan Jay Lerner
Music by Frederick Loewe

from *Camelot*

St. Genevieve! St. Genevieve!
It's Guenevere! Remember me?
St. Genevieve! St. Genevieve!
I'm over here beneath this tree.
You know how faithful and devout I am.
You must admit I've always been a lamb.

But Genevieve, St. Genevieve,
I won't obey you anymore!
You've gone a bit too far.
I won't be bid and bargain'd for
Like beads at a bazaar.

St. Genevieve, I've run away,
Eluded them and fled,
And from now on I intend to pray
To someone else instead.

Oh Genevieve, St. Genevieve,
Where were you when my youth was sold?
Dear Genevieve, sweet Genevieve,
Shan't I be young before I'm old?

Where are the simple joys of maidenhood?
Where are all those adoring, daring boys?
Where's the knight pining so for me
He leaps to death in woe for me?
Oh, where are a maiden's simple joys?

Shan't I have the normal life a maiden
    should?
Shall I never be rescued in the wood?
Shall two knights never tilt for me
And let their blood be spilt for me?
Oh, where are the simple joys of
    maidenhood?

Shall I not be on a pedestal,
Worshipped and competed for?
Not be carried off, or better st'll,
Cause a little war?

Where are the simple joys of maidenhood?
Are those sweet, gentle pleasures gone for
    good?
Shall a feud not begin for me?
Shall kith not kill their kin for me?
Oh, where are the trivial joys?
Harmless, convivial joys?
Where are the simple joys of maidenhood?

Sing for Your Supper

Words by Lorenz Hart
Music by Richard Rodgers

from *The Boys from Syracuse*

Hawks and crows do lots of things,
But the canary only sings.
She is a courtesan on wings—
So I've heard.
Eagles and storks are twice as strong.
All the canary knows is a song.
But the canary gets along—
Gilded bird!

Sing for your supper,
And you'll get breakfast.
Songbirds always eat
If their song is sweet to hear.
Sing for your luncheon,
And you'll get dinner.
Dine with wine of choice,
If romance is in your voice.
I heard from a wise canary
Trilling makes a fellow willing,
So, little swallow, swallow now.
Now is the time to
Sing for your supper,
And you'll get breakfast.
Songbirds are not dumb,
They don't buy a crumb
Of bread,
It's said.
So sing and you'll be fed.

Sit Down You're Rockin' the Boat

By Frank Loesser

from *Guys and Dolls*

I dreamed last night I got on the boat to heaven
And by some chance I had brought my dice along.
And there I stood and I hollered, "Someone fade me,"
But the passengers they knew right from wrong.

For the people all said, "Sit down,
Sit down, you're rockin' the boat;
And the devil will drag you under
By the sharp lapel of your checkered coat;
Sit down, sit down, sit down, sit down,
Sit down, you're rockin' the boat.

I sailed away on that little boat to heaven
And by some chance found a bottle in my fist.
And there I stood nicely passin' out the whiskey,
But the passengers were bound to resist.

For all the people said, "Beware,
Beware you'll scuttle the ship;
And the devil will drag you under
By the fancy tie 'round your wicked throat;
Sit down, sit down, sit down, sit down,
Sit down, you're rockin' the boat.

And as I laughed at those passengers to heaven
A great big wave came and washed me overboard.
And as I sank, and I hollered, "Someone save me,"
That's the moment I woke up, thank the Lord.

And I said to myself, "Sit down,
Sit down, you're rockin' the boat."
Said to myself, "Sit down, you're rockin' the boat."
And the devil will drag you under
With a soul so heavy you'd never float;
Sit down, sit down, sit down, sit down,
Sit down, you're rockin' the boat.

Sixteen Going on Seventeen

Lyrics by Oscar Hammerstein II
Music by Richard Rodgers

from *The Sound of Music*

You wait, little girl, on an empty stage
For fate to turn the light on.
Your life, little girl, is an empty page
That men will want to write on—
To write on.

You are sixteen, going on seventeen,
Baby, it's time to think.
Better beware,
Be canny and careful,
Baby, you're on the brink.

You are sixteen, going on seventeen,
Fellows will fall in line,
Eager young lads
And roués and cads
Will offer you food and wine.

Totally unprepared are you
To face a world of men.
Timid and shy and scared are you
Of things beyond your ken.

You need someone older and wiser
Telling you what to do…
I am seventeen, going on eighteen,
I'll take care of you.

I am sixteen, going on seventeen,
I know that I'm naïve.
Fellows I meet
May tell me I'm sweet
And willingly I'll believe.

I am sixteen, going on seventeen,
Innocent as a rose.
Bachelor dandies,
Drinkers of brandies—
What do I know of those?

Totally unprepared am I
To face a world of men,
Timid and shy and scared am I
Of things beyond my ken.

I need someone older and wiser
Telling me what to do…
You are seventeen, going on eighteen,
I'll depend on you.

REPRISE:
A bell is no bell till you ring it,
A song is no song till you sing it,
And love in your heart
Wasn't put there to stay—
Love isn't love
Till you give it away.

When you're sixteen, going on seventeen,
Waiting for life to start,
Somebody kind
Who touches your mind
Will suddenly touch your heart!

When that happens, after it happens,
Nothing is quite the same.
Somehow you know
You'll jump up and go
If ever he calls your name!

Gone are your old ideas of life,
The old ideas grow dim—
Lo and behold! You're someone's wife
And you belong to him!

You may think this kind of adventure
Never may come to you…
Darling sixteen-going-on-seventeen,
Wait—a year—or two.

A Sleepin' Bee

Lyric by Truman Capote and Harold Arlen
Music by Harold Arlen

from *House of Flowers*

When you're in love and you are wonderin'
If he really is the one.
There's an ancient sign sure to tell you
If your search is over and done.
Catch a bee and if he don't sting you,
You're in a spell that's just begun.
It's a guarantee till the end of time
Your true love you have won, have won.

When a bee lies sleepin'
In the the palm of your hand,
You're bewitched and deep in
Love's long looked after land.

Where you'll see a sun-up sky
With a mornin' new,
And where the days go laughin' by
As love comes a-callin' on you.

Sleep on, bee, don't waken,
Can't believe what just passed.
He's mine for the takin',
I'm so happy at last.

Maybe I dreams, but he seems
Sweet golden as a crown,
A sleepin' bee done told me,
I'll walks with feet off the groun'
When my one true love I has foun'.

Repeat Entire Song

Some People

Words by Stephen Sondheim
Music by Jule Styne

from *Gypsy*

Some people can get a thrill
Knitting sweaters and sitting still.
That's okay for some people
Who don't know they're alive!

Some people can thrive and bloom,
Living life in a living room.
That's perfect for some people,
Of one hundred and five!

But I at least gotta try,
When I think of all the sights that I gotta
   see yet,
All the places I gotta play,
All the things that I gotta be yet,
Come on, Poppa, whaddaya say?

Some people can be content
Playing Bingo and paying rent.
That's peachy for some people,
For some humdrum people to be.
But some people ain't me!

I had a dream,
A wonderful dream, Poppa!
All about June and Orpheum circuit,
Give me a chance and I know I can work it!

I had a dream,
Just as real as can be, Poppa!
There I was in Mister Orpheum's office,
And he was saying to me: "Rose!
Get yourself some new orchestrations,
New routines and red velvet curtains.
Get a feathered hat for the baby,
Photographs in front of the theatre.
Get an agent
And in jig time,
You'll be being booked in the big time!"

Oh, what a dream,
A wonderful dream, Poppa.
And all that I need is eighty-eight bucks,
   Poppa.
That's what he said, Poppa,
Only eighty-eight bucks.

Good-bye to blueberry pie!
Good riddance to all the socials I had to
   go to,
All the lodges I had to play,
All the Shriners I said hello to,
Hey, L.A., I'm coming your way!

Some people sit on their butts,
Got the dream, yeah, but not the guts!
That's living for some people,
For some humdrum people, I suppose.
Well, they can stay and rot,
But not Rose!

Someone Like You

Words by Leslie Bricusse
Music by Frank Wildhorn

from *Jekyll & Hyde*

I peered through the windows, watched life go by
Dreamed of tomorrow, but stayed inside.
The past was holding me, keeping life at bay.
I wandered, lost in yesterday,
Wanting to fly, but scared to try.

Then someone like you found someone like me.
And suddenly nothing is the same.
My heart's taken wing, I feel so alive,
'Cause someone like you found me.

It's like you took my dreams, made each one real,
You reached inside of me and made me feel.
And now I see a world I've never seen before.
Your love has opened every door;
You've set me free, now I can soar.

For someone like you found someone like me.
You touched my heart, nothing is the same.
There's a new way to live, a new way to love,
'Cause someone like you found me.

Oh, someone like you found someone like me.
And suddenly nothing will ever be the same.
My heart's taken wing, and I feel so alive,
'Cause someone like you loves me,
Loves me.

Someone Nice Like You

Words and Music by Leslie Bricusse and Anthony Newley

from the Musical Production *Stop the World—I Want to Get Off*

Why did someone nice like you, Evie [sweetheart],
Have to love someone like me?
When I think of all the men you could have loved,
The men you should have loved,
Who would have loved you,
You're worth so much more than me, Evie [sweetheart].
Believe you me, Evie [sweetheart],
You know that's true.
And if we could live twice,
I'd make life paradise,
For someone really nice like you.

You ask, why did someone nice like me
Have to love someone like you?
And you mention all the men I could have loved,
The men I should have loved,
Who would have loved me,
Maybe Sigmund Freud could tell you why
I'll love you till I die,
The way I do.
But who wants Freud's advice?
I'm sure it works with mice,
But not with someone nice like you.

Something Wonderful

Lyrics by Oscar Hammerstein II
Music by Richard Rodgers

from *The King and I*

This is a man who thinks with his heart,
His heart is not always wise.
This is a man who stumbles and falls,
But this is a man who tries.
This is a man you'll forgive and forgive,
And help and protect, as long as you live...

He will not always say
What you would have him say,
But now and then he'll say
Something wonderful.

The thoughtless things he'll do
Will hurt and worry you,
But now and then he'll do
Something wonderful.

He has a thousand dreams
That won't come true.
You know that he believes in them
And that's enough for you.
You'll always go along,
Defend him when he's wrong
And tell him, when he's strong
He is wonderful.
He'll always need your love—
And so he'll get your love—
A man who needs your love
Can be wonderful!

Sophisticated Lady

Words and Music by Duke Ellington, Irving Mills and Mitchell Parish

from *Sophisticated Ladies*

They say into your early life romance came
And this heart of yours burned a flame,
A flame that flickered one day
And died away.
Then, with disillusion deep in your eyes
You learned that fools in love soon grow wise.

The years have changed you, somehow
I see you now…
Smoking, drinking,
Never thinking of tomorrow,
Nonchalant.
Diamonds shining,
Dancing, dining
With some man in a restaurant.
Is that all you really want?
No, sophisticated lady,
I know
You miss the love you lost long ago,
And when nobody is nigh
You cry.

Speak Low

Words by Ogden Nash
Music by Kurt Weill

from the Musical Production *One Touch of Venus*

Speak low when you speak, love,
Our summer day withers away too soon, too soon.
Speak low when you speak, love,
Our moment is swift, like ships adrift,
We're swept adrift, too soon.

Speak low darling, speak low
Love is a spark lost in the dark too soon, too soon.
I feel wherever I go
That tomorrow is near,
Tomorrow is here and always too soon.

Time is so old and love is so brief,
Love is pure gold and time a thief.
We're late darling, we're late
The curtain descends,
Everything ends too soon, too soon,
I wait darling, I wait.
Will you speak low to me,
Speak love to me and soon.

Springtime for Hitler

Music and Lyrics by Mel Brooks

from *The Producers*

Germany was having trouble,
What a sad, sad story,
Needed a new leader to restore its former
   glory.
Where, oh where, was he?
Where could that man be?
We looked around and then we found
The man for you and me.

And now it's springtime for Hitler and
   Germany,
Deutschland is happy and gay,
We're marching to a faster pace,
Look out, here comes the master race.
Springtime for Hitler and Germany,
Rhineland's a fine land once more.
Springtime for Hitler and Germany,
Look out Europe, we're goin' on tour.

Springtime for Hitler and Germany,
Winter for Poland and France.
Springtime for Hitler and Germany,
Come on Germans, go into your dance!

Spoken:
I was born in Düsseldorf,
And that is why they call me Rolf.
Don't be stupid, be a smarty,
Come and join the Nazi party.

Sung:
And now it's springtime for Hitler and
   Germany,
Goosesteps, the new step today.
Bombs falling from the skies again,
Deutschland is on the rise again.

Springtime for Hitler and Germany,
U-boats are sailing once more.
Springtime for Hitler and Germany
Means that soon we'll be going,
We've got to be going,
You know we'll be going,
You bet we'll be going,
You know we'll be going to war!

Stepsisters' Lament

Lyrics by Oscar Hammerstein II
Music by Richard Rodgers

from *Cinderella*

Why would a fellow want a girl like her,
A frail and fluffy beauty?
Why can't a fellow ever once prefer
A solid girl like me?

She's a frothy little bubble
With a flimsy kind of charm,
And with very little trouble,
I could break her little arm!

Oh, oh, why would a fellow want a girl like her,
So obviously unusual?
Why can't a fellow ever once prefer
A usual girl like me?

Her cheeks are a pretty shade of pink,
But not any pinker than a rose is.
Her skin may be delicate and soft,
But not any softer than a doe's is.

Her neck is no whiter than a swan's.
She's only as dainty as a daisy.
She's only as graceful as a bird.
So why is the fellow going crazy?

Oh, why would a fellow want a girl like her,
A girl who's merely lovely?
Why can't a fellow ever once prefer
A girl who's merely me?
What's the matter with the man?
What's the matter with the man?
What's the matter with the man?

Summer Nights

Lyric and Music by Warren Casey and Jim Jacobs

from *Grease*

Boy: Summer lovin' had me blast.
Girl: Summer lovin' happened so fast.
Boy: Met a girl crazy for me.
Girl: Met a boy, cute as can be.

Summer days drifting away
To, uh, oh, those summer nights.

Well-a, well-a, well-a
Tell me more. Tell me more.
Did you get very far?
Tell me more. Tell me more.
Like, does he have a car?

Boy: She swam by me. She got a cramp.
Girl: He ran by me, got my suit damp.
Boy: Saved her life, she nearly drowned.
Girl: He showed of, splashing around.

Summer sun, something's begun
But, uh, oh, those summer nights.

Well-a, well-a, well-a uh.
Tell me more. Tell me more.
Was it love at first sight?
Tell me more. Tell me more.
Did she put up a fight?

Boy: Took her bowling in the arcade.
Girl: We went strolling; drank lemonade.
Boy: We made out under the dock.
Girl: We stayed out till ten o'clock.

Summer fling don't mean a thing
But uh, oh, those summer nights.

Tell me more, tell me more.
But you don't got to brag.
Tell me more, tell me more.
'Cause he sounds like a drag.
Shu-da bop bop. Shu-da bop bop.
Shu-da bop bop. Shu-da bop bop.

Girl: He got friendly, holding my hand.
Boy: She got friendly, down in the sand.
Girl: He was sweet; just turned eighteen.
Boy: She was good. You know what I mean.

Summer heat; boy and girl meet.
But, uh, oh those summer nights.

Tell me more. Tell me more.
How much dough did he spend?
Tell me more. Tell me more.
Could she get me a friend?

Girl: It turned colder; that's where it ends.
Boy: So I told her we'd still be friends.
Girl: Then we made our true love vow.
Boy: Wonder what she's doin' now.

Summer dreams
Ripped at the seams
But, oh, those summer nights.
Tell me more.
Tell me more.

The Sweetest Sounds

Lyrics and Music by Richard Rodgers

from *No Strings*

What do I really hear?
What is in the ear of my mind?
Which sounds are true and clear,
And which will never be defined?

The sweetest sounds I'll ever hear
Are still inside my head.
The kindest words I'll ever know
Are waiting to be said.
The most entrancing sight of all
Is yet for me to see.
And the dearest love in all the world
Is waiting somewhere for me.
Is waiting somewhere,
Somewhere for me.

Tell Me on a Sunday

Music by Andrew Lloyd Webber
Lyrics by Don Black

from *Song and Dance*

Don't write a letter when you want to leave.
Don't call me at 3 A.M. from a friend's
    apartment.
I'd like to choose
How I hear the news.
Take me to a park that's covered with trees.
Tell me on a Sunday, please.

Let me down easy, no big song and dance.
No long faces, no long looks, no deep
    conversation.
I know the way
We should spend the day.
Take me to a zoo that's got chimpanzees.
Tell me on a Sunday, please.

Don't want to know who's to blame,
It won't help knowing.
Don't want to fight
Day and night,
Bad enough you're going.

Don't leave me in silence with no words
    at all.
Don't get drunk and slam the door,
That's no way to end this.
I know how I want to say goodbye.
Find a circus ring with a flying trapeze.
Tell me on a Sunday, please.

I don't want to fight day and night,
Bad enough you're going.

Don't leave in silence with no words at all.
Don't get drunk and slam the door,
That's no way to end this.
I know how I want you to say goodbye.
Don't run off in the pouring rain.
Don't call me as they call your plane.
Take the hurt out of all the pain.
Take me to a park that's covered with trees.
Tell me on a Sunday, please.

Ten Cents a Dance

Words by Lorenz Hart
Music by Richard Rodgers

from *Simple Simon*

I work at the Palace Ballroom,
But gee, that place is cheap;
When I get back to my chilly hall room
I'm much too tired to sleep.
I'm one of those lady teachers,
A beautiful hostess, you know,
One that the palace features
At exactly a dime a throw.

Refrain:
Ten cents a dance;
That's what they pay me.
Gosh, how they weigh me down!
Ten cents a dance,
Pansies and rough guys,
Tough guys who tear my gown!
Seven to midnight, I hear drums,
Loudly the saxophone blows,
Trumpets are tearing my eardrums.
Customers crush my toes.
Sometimes I think I've found my hero
But it's a queer romance
All that you need is a ticket;
Come on, big boy, ten cents a dance!

Fighters and sailors and bowlegged tailors
Can pay for their tickets and rent me!
Butchers and barbers and rats from the
    harbors
Are sweethearts my good luck has sent me.
Though I've a chorus of elderly beaux
Stockings are porous with holes at the toes.
I'm here till closing time
Dance and be merry, it's only a dime.

Sometimes I think I've found my hero
But it's a queer romance,
All that you need is a ticket!
Come on, big boy, ten cents a dance!

Thank Heaven for Little Girls

Words by Alan Jay Lerner
Music by Frederick Loewe

from *Gigi*

Each time I see a little girl,
Of five, or six, or seven,
I can't resist a joyous urge
To smile and say:

Thank heaven for little girls!
For little girls get bigger ev'ry day.
Thank heaven for little girls!
They grow up in the most delightful way.

Those little eyes,
So helpless and appealing,
One day will flash,
And send you crashing through the ceiling.

Thank heaven for little girls.
Thank heaven for them all,
No matter where,
No matter who,
Without them what would little boys do?
Thank heaven,
Thank heaven.
Thank heaven for little girls.

Think of Me

Music by Andrew Lloyd Webber
Lyrics by Charles Hart
Additional Lyrics by Richard Stilgoe

from *The Phantom of the Opera*

Christine:
Think of me,
Think of me fondly when we've said
    goodbye.
Remember me,
Ev'ry so often, promise me you'll try.
On that day, that not so distant day,
When you are far away and free,
If you ever find a moment,
Spare a thought for me.

And though it's clear,
Though it was always clear,
That this was never meant to be,
If you happen to remember,
Stop and think of me.

Think of August,
When the trees were green.
Don't think about the way
Things might have been.

Think of me,
Think of me waking, silent and resigned.
Imagine me,
Trying too hard to put you from my mind.
Think of me, please say you'll think of me,
Whatever else you choose to do.
There will never be a day
When I won't think of you.

Raoul:
Can it be,
Can it be Christine?
Long ago,
It seems so long ago,
How young and innocent we were.
She may not remember me,
But I remember her.

Christine:
Flowers fade,
The fruits of summer fade,
They have their season, so do we.
But please promise me that sometimes,
You will think...of me!

This Can't Be Love

Words by Lorenz Hart
Music by Richard Rodgers

from *The Boys from Syracuse*

In Verona, my late cousin Romeo
Was three times as stupid as my Dromio.
For he fell in love
And then he died of it.
Poor half-wit!

Refrain:
This can't be love
Because I feel so well;
No sobs, no sorrows, no sighs.
This can't be love,
I get no dizzy spell,
My head is not in the skies.
My heart does not stand still;
Just hear it beat!
This is too sweet
To be love.
This can't be love
Because I feel so well,
But still I love to look in your eyes.

Though your cousin loved my cousin Juliet,
Loved her with a passion much more truly yet,
Some poor playwright
Wrote their drama just for fun.
It won't run!

Refrain

This Is the Moment

Words by Leslie Bricusse
Music by Frank Wildhorn

from *Jekyll & Hyde*

This is the moment, this is the day,
When I send all my doubts and demons on their way.
Every endeavor I have made ever come in into play,
Is here and now today.

This is the moment, this is the time
When the momentum and the moment are in rhyme.
Give me this moment, this precious chance.
I'll gather up my past and make some sense at last.

This is the moment when all I've done,
All of the dreaming, scheming and screaming become one!
This is the day, see it sparkle and shine,
When all I've lived for becomes mine!

For all these years I've faced the world alone,
And now the time has come
To prove to them I made it on my own.

This is the moment, my final test.
Destiny beckoned, I never reckoned second best.
I won't look down, I must not fall.
This is the moment, the sweetest moment of them all!

This is the moment. Damn all the odds.
This day or never, I'll sit forever with the gods!
When I look back, I will always recall,
Moment for moment, this was the moment,
The greatest moment of all.

This Nearly Was Mine

Lyrics by Oscar Hammerstein II
Music by Richard Rodgers

from *South Pacific*

One dream in my heart,
One love to be living for,
One love to be living for,
This nearly was mine.

One girl for my dream,
One partner in paradise,
This promise of paradise,
This nearly was mine.

Close to my heart she came,
Only to fly away,
Only to fly as day flies from moonlight.

Now, now I'm alone
Still dreaming of paradise,
Still saying that paradise
Once nearly was mine.

So clear and deep are my fancies
Of things I wish were true,
I'll keep remembering evenings
I wish I'd spent with you.

I'll keep remembering kisses
From lips I'll never own,
And all the lovely adventures
That we have never known.

Now, now I'm alone
Still dreaming of paradise,
Still saying that paradise
Once nearly was mine.

To Keep My Love Alive

Words by Lorenz Hart
Music by Richard Rodgers

from *A Connecticut Yankee*

I've been married and married,
And often I've sighed,
I'm never a bridesmaid,
I'm always the bride;
I never divorced them,
I hadn't the heart,
Yet, remember these sweet words,
"Till death do us part."

I married many men, a ton of them,
Because I was untrue to none of them,
Because I bumped off ev'ry one of them
To keep my love alive.

Sir Paul was frail, he looked a wreck to me.
At night he was a horse's neck to me,
So I performed an appendectomy,
To keep my love alive!

Sir Thomas had insomnia,
He couldn't sleep at night,
I bought a little arsenic,
He's sleeping now all right.

Sir Philip played the harp, I cussed the thing.
I crowned him with his harp to bust the
    thing,
And now he plays where harps are just the
    thing,
To keep my love alive,
To keep my love alive.

I thought Sir George had possibilities,
But his flirtations made me ill at ease,
And when I'm ill at ease, I kill at ease,
To keep my love alive.

Sir Charles came from a sanatorium,
And yelled for drinks in my emporium.
I mixed one drink, he's in memoriam,
To keep my love alive!

Sir Francis was a singing bird,
A nightingale,
That's why I tossed him off my balcony,
To see if he could fly.

Sir Athelstane indulged in fratricide,
He killed his dad and that was patricide.
One night I stabbed him by my mattress side,
To keep my love alive,
To keep my love alive.

Tomorrow

Lyric by Martin Charnin
Music by Charles Strouse

from the Musical Production *Annie*

The sun'll come out tomorrow,
Bet your bottom dollar that tomorrow,
There'll be sun!
Just thinkin' about tomorrow
Clears away the cobwebs and the sorrow,
'Til there's none!

Refrain:
When I'm stuck with a day that's gray and lonely,
I just stick out my chin and grin and say:
Oh, the sun'll come out tomorrow,
So ya gotta hang on 'til tomorrow,
Come what may!
Tomorrow, tomorrow,
I love ya, tomorrow,
You're always a day away!

Refrain

Tomorrow, tomorrow,
I love ya, tomorrow,
You're always a day away!

Too Close for Comfort

Words and Music by Jerry Bock, Larry Holofcener and George Weiss

from the Musical *Mr. Wonderful*

The men of science are a brilliant clan.
Just think, just think,
They can tell how far it is from here to a
   star above,
And yet they cannot measure the safest
   distance
Between a woman and man in love.
Since I cannot consult a book of knowledge
That may be lying on a shelf,
I guess I'll have a confidential discussion
   with myself.

Refrain:
Be wise, be smart,
Behave my heart,
Don't upset your cart
When she's [he's] so close.
Be soft, be sweet,
But be discreet,
Don't go off your beat.
She's [He's] too close for comfort.
Too close, too close for comfort,
Please not again.
Too close, too close to know
Just when to say, "when."

Be firm, be fair,
Be sure, beware,
On your guard, take care
While there's such temptation.
One thing leads to another,
Too late to run for cover,
She's [He's] much too close for
   comfort now!

Refrain

Too close, too close.
She's [He's] much too close for comfort
   now.

Triplets

Words by Howard Dietz
Music by Arthur Schwartz

from *Between the Devil*

Three little unexpected children,
Simultaneously the doctor brought us,
And you can see that we'll be three
Forever and aye (Ee-i-o).
You wouldn't know how agonizing
Being triple can be.
Each one is individually the victim
Of the clinical day (Ee-i-o).
Ev'ry summer we go away
To Baden Baden Baden.
Ev'ry winter we come back home
To Walla Walla (Walla).

Refrain:
We do ev'rything alike.
We look alike,
We dress alike,
We walk alike,
We talk alike,
And what is more,
We hate each other very much.
We hate our folks,
We're sick of jokes
On what an art
It is to tell us apart.

If one of us gets the measles,
Another one gets the measles,
Then all of us gets the measles,
And mumps and croup.
How I wish I had a gun,
A little gun,
It would be fun to shoot the other two,
And be only one.

Missus Whiffle Poofer loves
To talk to Missus Hildendorfer,
Of the fatal natal day
She had her silly Willie.
Missus Hassencooper loves
To talk to Missus Goldenwasser,
Of her major operation,
When she had her twins.
But when mother comes along,
She silences the others,
She accomplished something
That is very rare in mothers.
People who disparage marriage,
Burdened with a baby carriage,
Cater to the mater
And her large perambulator.
MGM has got a Leo,
But Mama has got a trio.
She is proud,
But says three is a crowd.

Refrain

We eat the same kind of vittels,
We drink the same kind of bottles,
We sut in the same kind of high chair.
(High chair, high chair.)
How I wish I had a gun,
A little gun,
It would be fun to shoot the other two
And be only one.

Too Darn Hot

Words and Music by Cole Porter

from *Kiss Me, Kate*

It's too darn hot,
It's too darn hot,
I'd like to sup with my baby tonight,
And play the pup with my baby tonight.
I'd like to sup with my baby tonight,
And play the pup with my baby tonight,
But I ain't up to my baby tonight
'Cause it's too darn hot.

It's too darn hot,
It's too darn hot,
I'd like to stop for my baby tonight,
And blow my top with my baby tonight.
I'd like to stop for my baby tonight,
And blow my top with my baby tonight,
But I'd be a flop with my baby tonight
'Cause it's too darn hot.

It's too darn hot,
It's too darn hot,
I'd like to fool with my baby tonight,
Break ev'ry rule with my baby tonight.
I'd like to fool with my baby tonight,
Break ev'ry rule with my baby tonight.
But pillow, you'll be my baby tonight
'Cause it's too darn hot.

According to the Kinsey report
Ev'ry average man you know
Much prefers to play his favorite sport
When the temperature is low,
But when the thermometer goes 'way up
And the weather is sizzling hot,
Mister Adam
For his madam
Is not.
'Cause it's too, too,
Too darn hot,
It's too darn hot,
It's too darn hot.

It's too darn hot,
It's too darn hot.
I'd like to call on my baby tonight,
And give my all to my baby tonight,
I'd like to call on my baby tonight,
And give my all to my baby tonight,
But I can't play ball with my baby tonight
'Cause it's too darn hot.

It's too darn hot,
It's too darn hot.
I'd like to meet with my baby tonight,
Get off my feet with my baby tonight,
I'd like to meet with my baby tonight,
Get off my feet with my baby tonight,
But no repeat with my baby tonight,
'Cause it's too darn hot.

It's too darn hot,
It's too darn hot.
I'd like to coo to my baby tonight,
And pitch the woo with my baby tonight,
I'd like to coo to my baby tonight,
And pitch the woo with my baby tonight,
But, brother, you bite my baby tonight,
'Cause it's too darn hot.

According to the Kinsey report,
Ev'ry average man you know
Much prefers to play his favorite sport
When the temperature is low,
But when the thermometer goes 'way up
And the weather is sizzling hot,
Mister Gob
For his squab,
A marine
For his queen,
A G.I.
For his cutie pie
Is not.
'Cause it's too, too,
Too darn hot.

Try to Remember

Words by Tom Jones
Music by Harvey Schmidt

from *The Fantasticks*

Try to remember the kind of September
When life was slow and oh, so mellow.
Try to remember the kind of September
When grass was green and grain was yellow.
Try to remember the kind of September
When you were a tender and callow fellow.
Try to remember and if you remember
Then follow.

Echo:
Follow, follow, follow, follow,
Follow, follow, follow, follow.

Try to remember when life was so tender
That no one wept except the willow.
Try to remember when life was so tender
That dreams were kept beside your pillow.
Try to remember when life was so tender
That love was an ember about to billow.
Try to remember and if you remember
Then follow.

Echo

Deep in December it's nice to remember
Although you know the snow will follow.
Deep in December it's nice to remember
Without a hurt the heart is hollow.
Deep in December, it's nice to remember
The fire of September that made us mellow.
Deep in December our hearts should remember
And follow.

Echo

Unexpected Song

Music by Andrew Lloyd Webber
Lyrics by Don Black

from *Song and Dance*

I have never felt like this,
For once I'm lost for words,
Your smile has really thrown me.
This is not like me at all,
I never thought I'd know
The kind of love you've shown me.

Refrain:
Now no matter where I am,
No matter what I do,
I see your face appearing
Like an unexpected song,
An unexpected song
That only we are hearing.

I don't know what's going on,
Can't work it out at all.
Whatever made you choose me?
I just can't believe my eyes,
You look at me as though
You couldn't bear to lose me.

Refrain

I have never felt like this.
For once I'm lost for words,
Your smile has really thrown me.
This is not like me at all,
I never thought I'd know
The kind of love you've shown me.

Now no matter where I am,
No matter what I do,
I see your appearing
Like an unexpected song,
An unexpected song
That only we are hearing.
Like an unexpected song,
An unexpected song
That only we are hearing.

We Go Together

Lyric and Music by Warren Casey and Jim Jacobs

from *Grease*

We go together,
Like ra-ma la-ma la-ma ka ding-a da ding-dong.
Remembered forever
As shoo-bop-sha-wad-da wad-da yip-pi-ty boom-de-boom.
Chang chang ah chan-it-ty chang-shoo bop.
That's the way it should be, wha oooh, yeah!
We're one of a kind
Like dip da dip da dip doo wop-a doo-bee doo,
Our names are signed
Boogedy boogedy boogedy boogedy shooby doo wop she bop.
Chang chang ah changitty chang-shoo bop,
We'll always bee-ee like one.
Wa wa wa waaah.

When we go out at night, and stars are shining bright
Up in the skies above.
Or at the high school dance, where you can find romance,
Maybe it might be love.

We're for each other
Like-a wop ba-ba lu-mop and wop bam boom.
Just like my brother
Is sha-na-na-na-na-na yip-pi-ty dip-de doom
Chang chang ah changitty-chang–shoo bop,
We'll always be together, together.

What I Did for Love

Music by Marvin Hamlisch
Lyric by Edward Kleban

from *A Chorus Line*

Kiss today goodbye,
The sweetness and the sorrow.
We did what we had to do,
And I can't regret
What I did for love,
What I did for love.

Look, my eyes are dry,
The gift was ours to borrow.
It's as if we always knew,
But I won't forget
What I did for love,
What I did for love.

Gone, love is never gone,
As we travel on,
Love's what we'll remember.

Kiss today goodbye
And point me toward tomorrow.
Wish me luck, the same to you.
Won't forget, can't regret
What I did for love.

What Kind of Fool Am I?

Words and Music by Leslie Bricusse and Anthony Newley

from the Musical Production *Stop the World—I Want to Get Off*

Refrain:
What kind of fool am I?
Who never fell in love,
It seems that I'm the only one
That I have been thinking of.
What kind of man is this?
An empty shell,
A lovely cell in which
An empty heart must dwell.

What kind of lips are these
That lied with every kiss?
That whispered empty words of love
That left me alone like this?
Why can't I fall in love
Like any other man
And maybe then I'll know
What kind of fool I am.

What kind of clown am I?
What do I know of life?
Why can't I cast away the mask
Of play and live my life?
Why can't I fall in love
'Til I don't give a damn
And maybe then I'll know
What kind of fool I am.

What'll I Do?

Words and Music by Irving Berlin

from *Music Box Revue of 1924*

Gone is the romance that was so divine.
'Tis broken and cannot be mended.
You must go your way and I must go mine.
But now that our love dreams have ended,

Refrain:
What'll I do when you are far away,
And I am blue, what'll I do?
What'll I do when I am wondering who
Is kissing you, what'll I do?
What'll I do with just a photograph
To tell my troubles to?
When I'm alone with only dreams of you,
That won't come true, what'll I do?

Do you remember a night filled with bliss?
The moonlight was softly descending.
Your lips and my lips were tied with a kiss.
A kiss with an unhappy ending.

Refrain

What's the Use of Wond'rin'

Lyrics by Oscar Hammerstein II
Music by Richard Rodgers

from *Carousel*

What's the use of wond'rin'
If he's good or if he's bad,
Or if you like the way he wears his hat?
Oh, what's the use of wond'rin'
If he's good or if he's bad?
He's your feller and you love him—
That's all there is to that.

Common sense may tell you
That the endin' will be sad
And now's the time to break and run away.
But what's the use of wond'rin'
If the endin' will be sad?
He's your feller and you love him—
There's nothin' more to say.

Somethin' made him the way that he is,
Whether he's false or true.
And somethin' gave him the things that are his—
One of those things is you.

So, when he wants your kisses
You will give them to the lad,
And anywhere he leads you you will walk.
And any time he needs you,
You'll go runnin' there like mad.
You're his girl and he's your feller—
And all the rest is talk.

When I'm Not Near the Girl I Love

Words by E.Y. Harburg
Music by Burton Lane

from *Finian's Rainbow*

Oh, my heart is beating wildly,
And it's all because you're here.
When I'm not near the girl I love,
I love the girl I'm near.

Ev'ry femme that flutters by me,
Is a flame that must be fanned.
When I can't fondle the hand I'm fond of,
I fondle the hand at hand.

My heart's in a pickle,
It's constantly fickle,
And not too particle, I fear.
When I'm not near the girl I love,
I love the girl I'm near.

What if they're tall and tender,
What if they're small and slender,
Long as they've got that gender,
I s'rrender.

Always I can't refuse 'em,
Always my feet pursues 'em,
Long as they've got a bosom,
I woo's 'em.

I'm confessing a confession,
And I hope I'm not verbose,
When I'm not close to the kiss that I cling to,
I cling to the kiss that's close.

As I'm more and more a mortal,
I am more and more a case.
When I'm not facing the face that I fancy,
I fancy the face I face.

For Sharon I'm carin',
But Suzan I'm choosin',
I'm faithful to whos'n is here.
When I'm not near the girl I love,
I love the girl I'm near.

When the Children Are Asleep

Lyrics by Oscar Hammerstein II
Music by Richard Rodgers

from *Carousel*

Mr. Snow:
I own a little house, and I sail a little boat,
And the fish I ketch I sell.
And in a manner of speakin' I'm doin'
  very well.
I love a little girl and she's in love with me.
And soon she'll be my bride.
And in a manner of speakin' I should be
  satisfied!
Carrie (Spoken):
Well, ain't you?

Mr. Snow:
If I told you my plans, and the things I
  intend,
It'd make ev'ry curl on yer head stand on
  end!

When I make enough money outa one little
  boat,
I'll put all my money in another little boat,
I'll make twic't as much outa two little boats,
And the fust thing you know, I'll have four
  little boats!

Then eight little boats, then a fleet of little
  boats!
Then a great, big fleet of great, big boats,
All ketchin' herrin, bringin' it to shore.
Sailin' out again and bringin' in more, and
  more and more
And more!

Carrie (Spoken):
Who's goin' t'eat all that herring?

Mr. Snow (Spoken):
They ain't goin' to be herring! Goin' to put
  them in cans
And call 'em sardines. Goin' to build a little
  sardine cannery—
Then a big one—then the biggest one in the
  country.
Carrie, I'm goin' t' get rich on sardines.
I mean we're goin' t'get rich—you and me,
  and all of us.

Mr. Snow (Sung):
The fust year we're married we'll hev one
  little kid,
The second year we'll go and hev another
  little kid,
You'll soon be darnin' socks fer eight
  little feet.
Carrie:
Are you buildin' up to another fleet?

Mr. Snow:
We'll build a lot more rooms,
Our dear little house'll get bigger,
Our dear little house'll get bigger!
Carrie:
And so will my figger.

Mr. Snow (Spoken):
Carrie, ken y'imagine how it'll be
When all the kids are upstairs in bed,
And you and me sit alone in the firelight?
Me in my armchair—you on my knee—
  mebbe?
Carrie (Spoken):
Mebbe.

Mr. Snow (Sung):
When the children are asleep, we'll sit and
  dream
The things that ev'ry other dad and mother
  dream.
When the children are asleep and lights are
  low,
If I still love you
The way I love you today,
You'll pardon my saying: "I told you so!"
When the children are asleep I'll dream with
  you.
We'll think, what fun we hev had
And be glad that it all came true!

Carrie:
When children are awake,
Arompin' thru the rooms and runnin' on the
  stairs,
Then in a manner of speakin'
A house is really theirs.
But once they close their eyes,
And we are left alone
And free from all their fuss,
Then in a manner of speakin'
We can be really us.

When the children are asleep,
(Dream all alone.)
We'll sit and dream,
(Dreams that won't be interrupted,)
The things that ev'ry other Dad and Mother
  dream
(Dreams that won't be interrupted,)

Mr. Snow:
When the children are asleep and lights are
  low.
(Lo! And behold.)

Carrie:
If I still love you
The way I love you today,
You'll pardon my saying: "I told you so!"
When the children are asleep I'll dream with
  you,
(You'll dream with me.)
We'll think what fun we hev had
And be glad that it all came true.

Mr. Snow:
When today is a long time ago.
Both:
You'll still hear me say that the best dream I
  know is:
Carrie:
When the children are asleep I'll dream with
  you!
Mr. Snow:
You!

Where, Oh Where

Words and Music by Cole Porter

from *Out of This World*

I often ask, because I feel
I've ev'ry right to ask,
Will time take on the task to reveal,
Yes or no, my beau ideal?
For even though, when I'm abed,
I dream he holds me tight,
Awake I never light,
On the man I plan, one day, to wed.

Where, oh where,
Is that combination so rare,
A cute knight in armor, completely a charmer,
Who'd still be a millionaire?

Where, oh where,
Is that combination so rare,
A youth who is able to wrap me in sable,
Who'd still be a love affair?

I could accept a cottage small,
By a roaring waterfall,
Yet I'd much prefer a castle cool,
By a marble swimming pool,

But where, oh where,
Is that combination so rare,
A highly admissible, kissable boy,
To fill me with, practic'lly kill me with joy,
Who'd still be a millionaire?
Tell me where, oh where, oh where?

Where Was I When They Passed Out the Luck?

Lyrics by Hal Hackady
Music by Larry Grossman

from *Minnie's Boys*

Where was I when they passed out brains?
Right at the head of the line.
Where was I when they passed out talent?
Right up front getting mine.
But when it came to the line
Where they handed out luck,
Where was your smart, clever friend?
Back, showin' off my talent and brains,
To the bums linin' up at the end.

Where was I when they passed out looks?
Needless to say I was there.
Who'll deny in the charm department,
I got more than my share.
But when the time rolled around,
And they handed out luck,
Where was your good-looking clown?
Off, tryin' out my profile and charm,
On a girl in a neighboring town!

I sure got a great sense of humor,
(Spoken) A-ha-ha!
(Sung) The day they were passing the pot.
I sure got a great sense of humor.
(Spoken) A-ha-ha!
(Sung) And I need all I got!

Where was I when they passed out guts?
Mister, I opened the store!
I'm the guy who invented chutzpah,
Show me a guy who's got more!
But when they yelled,
"Get your luck, 'cause it's runnin' out fast!
Step up and get your supply!"
Me, with my brains and talent and looks,
Blew the one thing you need to get by!
Where was I?

Who Will Love Me as I Am?

Words by Bill Russell
Music by Henry Krieger

from *Side Show*

Like a fish plucked from the ocean,
Tossed into a foreign stream,
Always knew that I was diff'rent,
Often fled into a dream.

I ignored the raging currents,
Right against the tide I swam.
But I floated with the question,
Who will love me as I am?

Like an odd exotic creature,
On display inside a zoo.
Hearing children asking questions
Makes me ask some questions, too.

Could we bend the laws of nature?
Could a lion love a lamb?
Who could see beyond this surface?
Who will love me as I am?

Refrain:
Who will ever call to say, "I love you"?
Send me flowers or a telegram,
Who could proudly stand beside me,
Who will love me as I am?

Like a clown whose tears cause laughter,
Trapped inside the center ring.
Even seeing smiling faces,
I am lonely pondering.

Who would want to join this madness?
Who would change my monogram?
Who will be part of my circus?
Who will love me as I am?

Refrain

Who could proudly stand beside me?
Who will love me as I am?

With One Look

Music by Andrew Lloyd Webber
Lyrics by Don Black and Christopher Hampton,
with contributions by Amy Powers

from *Sunset Boulevard*

With one look I can break your heart,
With one look I play every part.
I can make your sad heart sing,
With one look you'll know all you need to
   know.

With one smile I'm the girl next door
Or the love that you've hungered for.
When I speak it's with my soul
I can play any role.

No words can tell the stories my eyes tell,
Watch me when I frown, you can't write
   that down.
You know I'm right, it's there in black
   and white,
When I look your way you'll hear what I say.

Yes, with one look I put words to shame,
Just one look sets the screen aflame.
Silent music starts to play,
One tear in my eye makes the whole
   world cry.

With one look they'll forgive the past,
They'll rejoice I've returned at last
To my people in the dark,
Still out there in the dark.

Silent music starts to play.
With one look you'll know all you need
   to know.
With one look I'll ignite a blaze,
I'll return to my glory days.

They'll say Norma's back at last.
This time I'm staying for good,
I'll be back where I was born to be,
With one look I'll be me.

A Wonderful Day Like Today

Words and Music by Leslie Bricusse and Anthony Newley

from *The Roar of the Greasepaint—The Smell of the Crowd*

On a wonderful day like today
I defy any cloud to appear in the sky.
Dare any raindrop to plop in my eye
On a wonderful day like today.

On a wonderful morning like this
When the sun is as big as a yellow balloon
Even the sparrows are singing in tune
On a wonderful morning like this.

On a morning like this
I could kiss everybody
I'm so full of love and good will.
Let me say furthermore
I'd adore everybody
To come and dine.
The pleasure's mine.
And I will pay the bill.

May I take this occasion to say
That the whole human race should go down on its knees,
Show that we're grateful for mornings like these.
For the world's in a wonderful way
On a wonderful day like today.

A Wonderful Guy

Lyrics by Oscar Hammerstein II
Music by Richard Rodgers

from *South Pacific*

I expect every one
Of my crowd to make fun
Of my proud protestations of faith in
   romance,
And they'll say I'm naïve
As a babe to believe
Any fable I hear from a person in pants.

Fearlessly I'll face them and argue their
   doubts away.
Loudly I'll sing about flowers and spring.
Flatly I'll stand on my little flat feet and say,
Love is a grand and a beautiful thing!
I'm not ashamed to reveal
The world-famous feeling I feel.

I'm as corny as Kansas in August,
I'm as normal as blueberry pie.
No more a smart
Little girl with no heart,
I have found me a wonderful guy.
I am in a conventional dither
With a conventional star in my eye,
And you will note
There's a lump in my throat
When I speak of that wonderful guy.

I'm as trite and as gay
As a daisy in May,
A cliché coming true!
I'm bromidic and bright
As a moon-happy night
Pouring light on the dew.
I'm as corny as Kansas in August,
High as a flag on the Fourth of July!
If you'll excuse
An expression I use,
I'm in love,
I'm in love,
I'm in love,
I'm in love,
I'm in love with a wonderful guy!

You Can't Get a Man with a Gun

Words and Music by Irving Berlin

from the Stage Production *Annie Get Your Gun*

Oh, my mother was frightened by a shotgun,
   they say,
That's why I'm such a wonderful shot.
I'd be out in the cactus and I'd practice all
   day,
And now tell me what have I got?

I'm quick on the trigger,
With targets not much bigger
Than a pinpoint, I'm number one.
But my score with a feller
Is lower than a cellar,
Oh, you can't get a man with a gun.

When I'm with a pistol
I sparkle like a crystal,
Yes, I shine like the morning sun,
But I lose all my luster
When with a bronco buster,
Oh, you can't get a man with a gun.

Refrain:
With a gu-un,
With a gu-un,
No you can't get a man with a gun.

If I went to battle
With someone's herd of cattle,
You'd have steak when the job was done,
But if I shot the herder,
They'd holler bloody murder,
And you can't shoot a male
In the tail, like a quail,
Oh, you can't get a man with a gun.

I'm cool, brave and daring
To see a lion glaring,
When I'm out with my Remington,
But a look from a mister
Will raise a fever blister,
Oh, you can't get a man with a gun.

The gals with umbrellers
Are always out with fellers
In the rain or the blazing sun,
But a man never trifles
With gals who carry rifles,
Oh, you can't get a man with a gun.

Refrain

A man's love is mighty,
He'll even buy a nightie
For a gal who he thinks is fun,
But they don't buy pajamas
For pistol packin' mamas,
And you can't get a hug
From a mug with a slug,
Oh, you can't get a man with a gun.

You Rule My World

Words and Music by David Yazbek

from *The Full Monty*

Dave:
Look at you,
You're lying there.
I feel your milky skin,
Caress your silky hair.
For all these years you've been with me,
I tilt my chin and what I see is only you,
Not feet or knees.
You grumble and I stumble
Towards the Muenster cheese.
I'm in your spell, a chubby fool,
And anyone can tell you rule my world.
My world,
No matter what I do,
You rule my world.

Harold:
Look at you,
My life, my dream,
My lady with the eighty-dollar slumber
    cream,
The hundred dollar haircuts,
The novelty appliances we never use,
And all those shoes you bought,
For when we go on the Alaskan cruise.
My boat is sinking,
I don't care.
You're ev'rything I want,
You rule my world.
My world,
You're ev'rything I need.

Dave:
Anywhere you go I'll follow.
Anything you want I'll give you,
Anytime you feel hollow, don't worry.
I'll swallow it whole.

Harold:
Anywhere, I'll follow you.
Anything at all.
Don't feel hollow, don't worry,
I'll make you whole.

Harold:
Look at me and hold me hard.
A moment please,
Before they seize the Visa card!
'Cause I'd do anything to keep you,
You rule my world,
My world.

Dave:
Just take a look at me.
You'll never leave my side.
Why can't I let you go?
Why can't I just lose—
You rule my world,
My world.

Dave: Though I'm unemployed,
Harold: A tad depressed,
Dave: I'm overweight,
Harold: I'm overdressed,
Both: There's nothing I can do,
Both: You rule my world.
Dave: There's nothing I can do.

You Took Advantage of Me

Words by Lorenz Hart
Music by Richard Rodgers

from *Present Arms*

He:
In the spring when the feeling was chronic,
And my caution was leaving you flat,
I should have made use of the tonic,
Before you gave me "that!"
A mental deficient you'll grade me,
I've given you plenty of data.
You came, you saw and you slayed me,
And that-a is that-a!

Refrain:
I'm a sentimental sap, that's all.
What's the use of trying not to fall?
I have no will,
You've made your kill,
'Cause you took advantage of me!
I'm just like an apple on a bough,
And you're gonna shake me down somehow,
So what's the use, you've cooked my goose,
'Cause you took advantage of me!

I'm so hot and bothered that I don't know
My elbow from my ear;
I suffer something awful each time you go,
And much worse when you're near.
Here am I with all my bridges burned,
Just a babe in arms where you're concerned,
So lock the doors and call me your's
'Cause you took advantage of me!

She:
When a girl has the heart of a mother
It must go to someone of course;
It can't be a sister or brother
And so I loved my horse.
But horses are frequently silly,
Mine ran from the beach of Kaluta,
And left me alone for a filly,
So I-a picked you-a.

Refrain

You'll Never Walk Alone

Lyrics by Oscar Hammerstein II
Music by Richard Rodgers

from *Carousel*

When you walk through a storm, hold your head up high
And don't be afraid of the dark,
At the end of the storm is a golden sky
And the sweet silver song of a lark.

Walk on through the wind,
Walk on through the wind,
Walk on through the rain,
Tho' your dreams be tossed and blown,
Walk on, walk on, with hope in your heart,
And you'll never walk alone,
You'll never walk alone!

(I Wonder Why?) You're Just in Love

Words and Music by Irving Berlin

from the Stage Production *Call Me Madam*

Boy:
(Refrain 1)
I hear singing and there's no one there.
I smell blossoms and the trees are bare.
All day long I seem to walk on air,
I wonder why.
I wonder why.
I keep tossing in my sleep at night,
And what's more I've lost my appetite.
Stars that used to twinkle in the skies,
Are twinkling in my eyes,
I wonder why.

Girl:
(Refrain 2)
You don't need analyzing,
It is not so surprising,
That you feel very strange but nice.
Your heart goes pitter patter,
I know just what's the matter,
Because I've been there once or twice.
Put your head on my shoulder,
You need someone who's older,
A rub down with a velvet glove.
There is nothing you can take
To relieve that pleasant ache.
You're not sick, you're just in love.

Boy:
Refrain 1

Girl:
Refrain 2

Show Index

Aida
60 Elaborate Lives

Ain't Misbehavin'
78 Honeysuckle Rose
96 I'm Gonna Sit Right Down and
      Write Myself a Letter
115 The Joint Is Jumpin'

Annie
86 I Don't Need Anything but You
114 It's the Hard-Knock Life
136 Maybe
203 Tomorrow

Annie Get Your Gun
71 The Girl That I Marry
144 My Defenses Are Down
224 You Can't Get a Man with a Gun

Anything Goes
118 Kate the Great

As Thousands Cheer
59 Easter Parade

Babes in Arms
94 I Wish I Were in Love Again
146 My Funny Valentine

**Beauty and the Beast:
The Broadway Musical**
26 Beauty and the Beast
68 Gaston
100 If I Can't Love Her

Bells Are Ringing
124 Long Before I Knew You
164 The Party's Over

Between the Devil
37 By Myself
205 Triplets

Big River
167 River in the Rain

The Boys from Syracuse
63 Falling in Love with Love
180 Sing for Your Supper
199 This Can't Be Love

By Jupiter
152 Nobody's Heart

Cabaret
44 Cabaret
85 I Don't Care Much
104 If You Could See Her
137 Maybe This Time

Call Me Madam
111 It's a Lovely Day Today
228 (I Wonder Why?) You're Just
      in Love

Camelot
81 How to Handle a Woman
179 The Simple Joys of Maidenhood

Can-Can
43 C'est Magnifique
50 Come Along with Me
112 It's All Right with Me

Carousel
214 What's the Use of Wond'rin'
216 When the Children Are Asleep
227 You'll Never Walk Alone

Chicago
15 And All That Jazz
48 Class

A Chorus Line
161 One
211 What I Did for Love

Cinderella
57 Do I Love You Because You're
      Beautiful?
106 In My Own Little Corner
192 Stepsisters' Lament

Company
16 Another Hundred People
24 Barcelona
28 Being Alive

A Connecticut Yankee
202 To Keep My Love Alive

Dearest Enemy
77 Here in My Arms

Do I Hear a Waltz?
56 Do I Hear a Waltz?

Do Re Mi
10 Adventure
128 Make Someone Happy

Dubarry Was a Lady
38 But in the Morning, No
72 Give Him the Oo-La-La
107 It Ain't Etiquette
108 It Was Written in the Stars

The Fantasticks
208 Try to Remember

Finian's Rainbow
79 How Are Things in Glocca Morra
103 If This Isn't Love
156 Old Devil Moon
215 When I'm Not Near the Girl
      I Love

Flower Drum Song
88 I Enjoy Being a Girl

Follies
35 Broadway Baby
125 Losing My Mind
170 The Road You Didn't Take

The Full Monty
34 Breeze off the River
225 You Rule My World

Funny Girl
58 Don't Rain on My Parade

**A Funny Thing Happened
on the Way to the Forum**
53 Comedy Tonight

The Garrick Gaieties
132 Manhattan
140 Mountain Greenery

Gentlemen Prefer Blondes
42 Bye Bye Baby
54 Diamonds Are a Girl's Best
      Friend

Gigi
92 I Remember It Well
197 Thank Heaven for Little Girls

The Girl Friend
29 The Blue Room

The Golden Apple
119 Lazy Afternoon

Grease
193 Summer Nights
210 We Go Together

The Great Magoo
113 It's Only a Paper Moon

Guys and Dolls
8 Adelaide's Lament
99 I've Never Been in Love Before
102 If I Were a Bell
127 Luck Be a Lady
147 My Time of Day
181 Sit Down You're Rockin'
      the Boat

Gypsy
61 Everything's Coming Up Roses
121 Let Me Entertain You
185 Some People

Songwriter Index

More Collections from The Lyric Library

BROADWAY VOLUME I

An invaluable collection of lyrics to 200 top Broadway tunes, including: All at Once You Love Her • All I Ask of You • And All That Jazz • Any Dream Will Do • As Long As He Needs Me • At the End of the Day • Autumn in New York • Bali Ha'i • Bewitched • Cabaret • Castle on a Cloud • Climb Ev'ry Mountain • Comedy Tonight • Don't Rain on My Parade • Everything's Coming up Roses • Hello, Dolly! • I Could Have Danced All Night • I Dreamed a Dream • I Remember It Well • If I Were a Bell • It's the Hard-Knock Life • Let Me Entertain You • Mame • My Funny Valentine • Oklahoma • Seasons of Love • September Song • Seventy Six Trombones • Shall We Dance? • Springtime for Hitler • Summer Nights • Tomorrow • Try to Remember • Unexpected Song • What I Did for Love • With One Look • You'll Never Walk Alone • (I Wonder Why?) You're Just in Love • and more.

_____00240201 ....$14.95

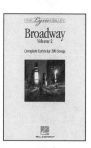

BROADWAY VOLUME II

200 more favorite Broadway lyrics (with no duplication from Volume I): Ain't Misbehavin' • All of You • Another Op'nin', Another Show • As If We Never Said Goodbye • Beauty School Dropout • The Best of Times • Bring Him Home • Brotherhood of Man • Camelot • Close Every Door • Consider Yourself • Do-Re-Mi • Edelweiss • Getting to Know You • Have You Met Miss Jones? • I Loved You Once in Silence • I'm Flying • If Ever I Would Leave You • The Impossible Dream (The Quest) • It Only Takes a Moment • The Lady Is a Tramp • The Last Night of the World • A Little More Mascara • Lost in the Stars • Love Changes Everything • Me and My Girl • Memory • My Heart Belongs to Daddy • On a Clear Day (You Can See Forever) • On My Own • People • Satin Doll • The Sound of Music • Sun and Moon • The Surrey with the Fringe on Top • Unusual Way (In a Very Unusual Way) • We Kiss in a Shadow • We Need a Little Christmas • Who Will Buy? • Wishing You Were Somehow Here Again • Younger Than Springtime • and more.

_____00240205 ....$14.95

CHRISTMAS

200 lyrics to the most loved Christmas songs of all time, including: Angels We Have Heard on High • Auld Lang Syne • Away in a Manger • Baby, It's Cold Outside • The Chipmunk Song • The Christmas Shoes • The Christmas Song (Chestnuts Roasting on an Open Fire) • Christmas Time Is Here • Do They Know It's Christmas? • Do You Hear What I Hear • Feliz Navidad • The First Noel • Frosty the Snow Man • The Gift • God Rest Ye Merry, Gentlemen • Goin' on a Sleighride • Grandma Got Run over by a Reindeer • Happy Xmas (War Is Over) • He Is Born, the Holy Child (Il Est Ne, Le Divin Enfant) • The Holly and the Ivy • A Holly Jolly Christmas • (There's No Place Like) Home for the Holidays • I Heard the Bells on Christmas Day • I Wonder As I Wander • I'll Be Home for Christmas • I've Got My Love to Keep Me Warm • In the Bleak Midwinter • It Came upon the Midnight Clear • It's Beginning to Look like Christmas • It's Just Another New Year's Eve • Jingle Bells • Joy to the World • Mary, Did You Know? • Merry Christmas, Darling • The Most Wonderful Time of the Year • My Favorite Things • Rudolph the Red-Nosed Reindeer • Silent Night • Silver Bells • The Twelve Days of Christmas • What Child Is This? • What Made the Baby Cry? • Wonderful Christmastime • and more.

_____00240206 ....$14.95

See our website for a complete contents list for each volume:
www.halleonard.com

FOR MORE INFORMATION, SEE YOUR LOCAL MUSIC DEALER,
OR WRITE TO:

HAL•LEONARD®
CORPORATION
7777 W. BLUEMOUND RD. P.O. BOX 13819 MILWAUKEE, WI 53213

Prices, contents and availability subject to change without notice.

More Collections from The Lyric Library

CLASSIC ROCK

Lyrics to 200 essential rock classics songs, including: All Day and All of the Night • All Right Now • Angie • Another One Bites the Dust • Back in the U.S.S.R. • Ballroom Blitz • Barracuda • Beast of Burden • Bell Bottom Blues • Brain Damage • Brass in Pocket • Breakdown • Breathe • Bus Stop • California Girls • Carry on Wayward Son • Centerfold • Changes • Cocaine • Cold As Ice • Come Sail Away • Come Together • Crazy Little Thing Called Love • Crazy on You • Don't Do Me like That • Don't Fear the Reaper • Don't Let the Sun Go down on Me • Don't Stand So Close to Me • Dreamer • Drive My Car • Dust in the Wind • 867-5309/Jenny • Emotional Rescue • Every Breath You Take • Every Little Thing She Does Is Magic • Eye in the Sky • Eye of the Tiger • Fame • Forever Young • Fortress Around Your Heart • Free Ride • Give a Little Bit • Gloria • Godzilla • Green-Eyed Lady • Heartache Tonight • Heroes • Hey Joe • Hot Blooded • I Fought the Law • I Shot the Sheriff • I Won't Back Down • Instant Karma • Invisible Touch • It's Only Rock 'N' Roll (But I like It) • It's Still Rock and Roll to Me • Layla • The Logical Song • Long Cool Woman (In a Black Dress) • Love Hurts • Maggie May • Me and Bobby McGee • Message in a Bottle • Mississippi Queen • Money • Money for Nothing • My Generation • New Kid in Town • Nights in White Satin • Paradise by the Dashboard Light • Piano Man • Rebel, Rebel • Refugee • Rhiannon • Roxanne • Shattered • Smoke on the Water • Sultans of Swing • Sweet Emotion • Walk This Way • We Gotta Get Out of This Place • We Will Rock You • Wouldn't It Be Nice • and many more!
_____00240183 ....$14.95

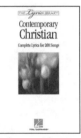

CONTEMPORARY CHRISTIAN

An amazing collection of 200 lyrics from some of the most prominent Contemporary Christian artists: Abba (Father) • After the Rain • Angels • Awesome God • Breathe on Me • Circle of Friends • Doubly Good to You • Down on My Knees • El Shaddai • Father's Eyes • Friends • Give It Away • Go Light Your World • God's Own Fool • Grand Canyon • The Great Adventure • The Great Divide • He Walked a Mile • Heaven and Earth • Heaven in the Real World • His Strength Is Perfect • Household of Faith • How Beautiful • I Surrender All • Jesus Freak • Joy in the Journey • Judas' Kiss • A Little More • Live Out Loud • Love Will Be Our Home • A Maze of Grace • The Message • My Utmost for His Highest • Oh Lord, You're Beautiful • People Need the Lord • Pray • Say the Name • Signs of Life • Speechless • Stand • Steady On • Via Dolorosa • The Warrior Is a Child • What Matters Most • Would I Know You • and more.
_____00240184 ....$14.95

COUNTRY

A great resource of lyrics to 200 of the best country songs of all time, including: Act Naturally • All My Ex's Live in Texas • All the Gold in California • Always on My Mind • Amazed • American Made • Angel of the Morning • Big Bad John • Blue • Blue Eyes Crying in the Rain • Boot Scootin' Boogie • Breathe • By the Time I Get to Phoenix • Could I Have This Dance • Crazy • Daddy's Hands • D-I-V-O-R-C-E • Down at the Twist and Shout • Elvira • Folsom Prison Blues • Friends in Low Places • The Gambler • Grandpa (Tell Me 'Bout the Good Old Days) • Harper Valley P.T.A. • He Thinks He'll Keep Her • Hey, Good Lookin' • I Fall to Pieces • I Hope You Dance • I Love a Rainy Night • I Saw the Light • I've Got a Tiger by the Tail • Islands in the Stream • Jambalaya (On the Bayou) • The Keeper of the Stars • King of the Road • Lucille • Make the World Go Away • Mammas Don't Let Your Babies Grow up to Be Cowboys • My Baby Thinks He's a Train • Okie from Muskogee • Ring of Fire • Rocky Top • Sixteen Tons • Stand by Me • There's a Tear in My Beer • Walkin' After Midnight • When You Say Nothing at All • Where the Stars and Stripes and the Eagle Fly • Where Were You (When the World Stopped Turning) • You Are My Sunshine • Your Cheatin' Heart • and more.
_____00240204 ....$14.95

See our website for a complete contents list for each volume:
www.halleonard.com

FOR MORE INFORMATION, SEE YOUR LOCAL MUSIC DEALER,
OR WRITE TO:

HAL•LEONARD®
CORPORATION
7777 W. BLUEMOUND RD. P.O. BOX 13819 MILWAUKEE, WI 53213

Prices, contents and availability subject to change without notice.

More Collections from The Lyric Library

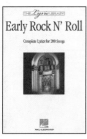

EARLY ROCK 'N' ROLL

Lyrics to 200 top songs that started the rock 'n' roll revolution, including: All I Have to Do Is Dream • All Shook Up • At the Hop • Baby Love • Barbara Ann • Be-Bop-A-Lula • Big Girls Don't Cry • Blue Suede Shoes • Bo Diddley • Book of Love • Calendar Girl • Chantilly Lace • Charlie Brown • Crying • Dancing in the Street • Do Wah Diddy Diddy • Don't Be Cruel (To a Heart That's True) • Earth Angel • Fun, Fun, Fun • Great Balls of Fire • He's a Rebel • Heatwave (Love Is like a Heatwave) • Hello Mary Lou • Hound Dog • I Walk the Line • It's My Party • Kansas City • The Loco-Motion • My Boyfriend's Back • My Guy • Oh, Pretty Woman • Peggy Sue • Rock and Roll Is Here to Stay • Sixteen Candles • Splish Splash • Stand by Me • Stupid Cupid • Surfin' U.S.A. • Teen Angel • A Teenager in Love • Twist and Shout • Walk like a Man • Where the Boys Are • Why Do Fools Fall in Love • Willie and the Hand Jive • and more.
_____00240203 ....$14.95

LOVE SONGS

Lyrics to 200 of the most romantic songs ever written, including: All My Loving • Always in My Heart (Siempre En Mi Corazon) • And I Love Her • Anniversary Song • Beautiful in My Eyes • Call Me Irresponsible • Can You Feel the Love Tonight • Cheek to Cheek • (They Long to Be) Close to You • Could I Have This Dance • Dedicated to the One I Love • Don't Know Much • Dream a Little Dream of Me • Endless Love • Fields of Gold • For Once in My Life • Grow Old with Me • The Hawaiian Wedding Song (Ke Kali Nei Au) • Heart and Soul • Hello, Young Lovers • How Deep Is the Ocean (How High Is the Sky) • I Just Called to Say I Love You • I'll Be There • I've Got My Love to Keep Me Warm • Just the Way You Are • Longer • L-O-V-E • Love Will Keep Us Together • Misty • Moonlight in Vermont • More (Ti Guardero' Nel Cuore) • My Funny Valentine • My Heart Will Go on (Love Theme from 'Titanic') • She • Speak Softly, Love (Love Theme) • Till • A Time for Us (Love Theme) • Unchained Melody • Up Where We Belong • We've Only Just Begun • What the World Needs Now Is Love • When I Fall in Love • Witchcraft • Wonderful Tonight • You Are the Sunshine of My Life • You're the Inspiration • You've Made Me So Very Happy • and more!
_____00240186 ....$14.95

POP/ROCK BALLADS

Lyrics to 200 top tunes of the pop/rock era, including: Adia • After the Love Has Gone • Against All Odds (Take a Look at Me Now) • Always on My Mind • Amazed • And So It Goes • Baby What a Big Surprise • Ben • Breathe • Change the World • Come to My Window • Do You Know Where You're Going To? • Don't Cry Out Loud • Don't Fall in Love with a Dreamer • Don't Let Me Be Lonely Tonight • Easy • Feelings (?Dime?) • Fire and Rain • From a Distance • Georgia on My Mind • Hero • I Hope You Dance • Imagine • In the Air Tonight • Iris • Just My Imagination (Running Away with Me) • Killing Me Softly with His Song • Laughter in the Rain • Looks like We Made It • My Heart Will Go on (Love Theme from 'Titanic') • New York State of Mind • The Rainbow Connection • Rainy Days and Mondays • Sailing • She's Always a Woman • Sing • Sunshine on My Shoulders • Take Me Home, Country Roads • Tears in Heaven • There You'll Be • Time After Time • Vision of Love • The Way We Were • Woman in Love • You're the Inspiration • You've Got a Friend • and more.
_____00240187 ....$14.95

See our website for a complete contents list for each volume:
www.halleonard.com

FOR MORE INFORMATION, SEE YOUR LOCAL MUSIC DEALER,
OR WRITE TO:

HAL•LEONARD®
CORPORATION
7777 W. BLUEMOUND RD. P.O. BOX 13819 MILWAUKEE, WI 53213

Prices, contents and availability subject to change without notice.